« *Words To Live By* »

Also by Eknath Easwaran

《》

Gandhi the Man

The Bhagavad Gita for Daily Living

Meditation

Mantram Handbook

Dialogue with Death

The Supreme Ambition

God Makes the Rivers to Flow

A Man to Match His Mountains

Love Never Faileth

Conquest of Mind

Original Goodness

The Constant Companion

The Compassionate Universe

《》

Classics of Indian Spirituality Series:

The Bhagavad Gita

The Dhammapada

The Upanishads

WORDS TO
« *LIVE BY* »

Inspiration for Every Day

E K N A T H   E A S W A R A N

N I L G I R I   P R E S S

I S B N : cloth, 0–915132–63–x; paper, 0–915132–62–1

Third printing May 1993

The Blue Mountain Center of Meditation, founded in
Berkeley in 1960 by Eknath Easwaran, publishes books on
how to lead the spiritual life in the home and the
community. For information please write to
Nilgiri Press, Box 477, Petaluma, California 94953

Printed on recycled, permanent paper

☉ The paper used in this publication meets the minimum
requirements of American National Standard for
Information Services – Permanence of Paper for Printed
Library Materials, ANSI Z39.48-1984.

Library of Congress Cataloging-in-Publication Data:
Easwaran, Eknath.
Words to live by : inspiration for every day
by Eknath Easwaran.

p.   cm.

I S B N 0–915132–63–x (alk. paper) : $18.00.

I S B N 0–915132–62–1 (pbk. : alk. paper) : $8.95

1. Devotional calendars. 2. Spiritual life. I. Title.

BL624.E19 1990

291.4'3 —dc20   90–39094

CIP

« *TABLE OF CONTENTS* »

To live at our best, each day we must renew our commitments, find strength to face challenges, and draw inspiration from a living source. This book of daily readings is meant to help us face the challenges and opportunities of every day.

The insights into daily life given here are stated in simple words. The emphasis is on practice, not on theory. Some of the suggestions concern the spiritual foundations of our lives, some are on a much more mundane level. But they all form a beautiful whole in practice, a unified approach to life. No one religion is emphasized. Inspiration is drawn from all the world's great religions – though it is not necessary for us to be religious in the conventional sense for this book to speak to our needs. All that is required is an open mind and a desire to know ourselves.

To use this book, read the entry for the day, reflect on it, and then recall it to mind now and then during the day. Try to bring its message into your life day by day.

It is not necessary to begin reading on January 1st, though the beginning entries are introductory. The book is designed so that we can pick it up and begin at any time of the year. Basic concepts are repeated at intervals throughout the year to support the continuity of our inner life. We can return to this collection year after year, each reading taking the inspiration deeper into our hearts.

Taken from the talks and writings of Eknath Easwaran, the readings stress his eight-point program for meditation and spiritual living. A detailed description of the eight-point program has been included at the end of the book. To begin with, it is enough to know that the program is based on the practice of meditation and the repetition of the mantram or Holy Name.

For those already acquainted with Easwaran's books, the readings will serve as reminders of familiar themes. Those who have not read Easwaran before will find a warm introduction here. For those who want to read more, we recommend *Meditation* and *The Mantram Handbook*. A complete list of books suitable for spiritual reading can be found at the back of the book.

As we go through the year with Easwaran, we take a new step on the path every day. Some days will be blessed with happiness and some will be marked by hardship, but each day can further our journey. One day at a time is enough.

— THE EDITORS

We are formed and molded by our thoughts.
Those whose minds are shaped by
selfless thoughts give joy when they speak
or act. Joy follows them like a shadow
that never leaves them.

THE BUDDHA

The method of meditation presented in this book involves sitting quietly with eyes closed and going slowly, in the mind, through the words of an inspirational passage that appeals to you deeply. It may be a prayer, or a poem from one of the great mystics, or a piece of scripture from any of the world's religions. It must be a very positive selection. When you sit quietly like this every morning, concentrating completely on words that embody your highest ideals, you are giving your mind thoughts of the purest quality to work with during the day. These selfless thoughts begin to mold your life. Joy begins to follow you throughout the day.

*If we had to seek for virtue outside of
ourselves, that would assuredly be difficult;
but as it is within us, it suffices to avoid bad
thoughts and to keep our souls turned
towards the Lord.*

PHILOKALIA

*Be ye therefore perfect, even as
your Father which is in heaven is perfect.*

THE GOSPEL ACCORDING TO
SAINT MATTHEW

To remake ourselves, we don't have to bring
goodness, love, fearlessness, and the like from
without and stuff them all into ourselves somehow. They are already present in us, deep in our
consciousness; that is why we can never really
rest content with being anything less than perfect. If we work to remove the impediments that
have built up over many years of conditioning,
to dislodge all the old resentments and fears and
selfish desires, our life will become like a fountain of living waters, as it was meant to be.

An old fountain may be so clogged with rub-
bish that not a drop of water can get through.
But with a lot of cleaning, you can get the water
to start playing again. Then grass and flowers
will grow around it, and birds will come there to
have their bath. Just so, love can flow from us as
from a living fountain, and those we live and
work with will come to us to be refreshed.

Familiar acts are beautiful through love.
PERCY BYSSHE SHELLEY

Through meditation and by giving full attention to one thing at a time, we can learn to direct attention where we choose. Simple, yet essential to the practice of love! Being one-pointed means we can give the person we are with our complete attention, even if she is contradicting our opinion on tax reform or explaining the peculiarities of Akkadian tablets. Once we can do this, boredom disappears from our relationships. People are not boring; we get bored because our attention wanders. When we can give someone our full attention, our attitude says clearly, "You matter to me. You have my respect."

*Try to treat with equal love all the people
with whom you have relations. Thus
the abyss between 'myself' and 'yourself'
will be filled in, which is the goal of
all religious worship.*

ANANDAMAYI MA

Love is a skill, a precious skill that can be learned. There are many other skills that are useful, even necessary, but in the end, nothing less than learning to love will satisfy us.

The saints and mystics tell us that life has only one overriding purpose: to discover the source of infinite love and then to express this love in daily living. Without love, life is empty; without love, life is meaningless. The only purpose which can satisfy us completely, fulfill all our desires, and then make our life a gift to the whole world, is the gradual realization of the Self within, which throws open the gates of love. We cannot dream what depth and breadth of love we are capable of until we make the discovery that this divine spark lives in every creature.

*The seed of God is in us. Given an intelligent
and hard-working farmer, it will thrive and
grow up to God, whose seed it is; and
accordingly its fruits will be God-nature.
Pear seeds grow into pear trees, nut seeds
into nut trees, and God seed into God.*

MEISTER ECKHART

The Lord is the seed of creativity in every being.
This seed does not need to be planted on a particular date, for it is already within us. It is indestructible. In the depths of the Dakota winter, the God-seed can thrive; in the heat of Death Valley it can still flourish. No matter what our past has been, no matter how many mistakes we have made, the God-seed is still intact.

When at last we begin to search for it we discover it is covered with weeds – weeds of fear and anger, giant thistles of greed. We shouldn't feel discouraged by the weeds. Once we take to meditation the weeds begin to wither and droop, and finally they fall to enrich the soil where the God-seed is growing. This God-seed within us will grow into a God-tree of love and service if we nurture it carefully.

*The soul is made of love and must ever strive
to return to love. Therefore, it can never find
rest nor happiness in other things. It must
lose itself in love. By its very nature it
must seek God, who is love.*

MECHTHILD OF MAGDEBURG

Spiritual fulfillment is an evolutionary imperative. There comes a time in the growth of civili-
zations, as with individuals, when the life-and-
death questions of material existence have been
answered, yet the soul still thirsts and physical
challenges cease to satisfy. Then we stand at a
crossroads: for without meaningful aspiration,
the human being turns destructive. Like a snake
that must shed its skin to grow, our industrial
civilization must shed its material outlook or
strangle in outgrown ideals whose constructive
potential has been spent.

*Genius . . . means little more than the
faculty of perceiving in an inhabitual way.*

WILLIAM JAMES

Attention is very much like a searchlight, and it
should be mounted in such a way that it can be
trained on any subject freely. When we are
caught up in some compulsion, this searchlight
has become stuck. After many years of being
stuck like this, it is hard to believe that the light
can turn. We think that the compulsion has become a permanent part of our personality. But
gradually, we can learn to work our attention
loose.

As an experiment, try to work cheerfully at
some job you dislike: you are training your attention to go where you want. Whatever you
do, give it your best concentration. Another
good exercise is learning to drop what you are
doing and shift your attention to something else
when the situation demands. For example,
when you leave your office, leave your work
there, too. Don't bring it to the dining table like
an untrained dog, barking at your heels.

All this is the spiritual equivalent of kicking
exercises in a dance lesson or knee bends in an
aerobics class. By practicing these exercises,
anybody can learn to direct attention freely.

*In deep meditation the flow of concentration
is continuous like the flow of oil.*

PATANJALI

There are two basic tools for mastering the thinking process. The first is meditation, which is described in the Hindu scriptures with a beautifully precise image: there should be a smooth, unbroken flow of attention on a single subject, like the flow of oil poured from one vessel to another. My method of meditation is to make the mind go slowly through the words of a particular passage from the scriptures or great mystics, as slowly as possible. Whenever the mind wants to slip off on another line of thought, bring the attention back to the words of the passage. It may take years, but eventually thought flows smoothly without interruption.

The other tool is the mantram – a short, powerful spiritual formula. Meditation slows down the thinking process; the mantram keeps it from acting from conditioning and speeding up again during the day. The mantram keeps the stream of concentrated thought flowing throughout the day.

We are what our thoughts have made us;
so take care about what you think. Words are
secondary. Thoughts live; they travel far.
SWAMI VIVEKANANDA

The ancestor of every destructive action, every destructive decision, is a negative thought. We do not have to be afraid of negative thoughts as long as we do not welcome them. They are in the air, and they may knock at anyone's door; but if we do not embrace them, ask them in, and make them our own, they can have no power over us.

We can think of thoughts as hitchhikers. In Berkeley, we used to see a lot of hitchhikers carrying signs: "Vancouver," "Mexico," "L.A." One said in simple desperation, "Anywhere!" Thoughts are a lot like those hitchhikers. We can pick them up or pass them by. Negative thoughts carry signs, but usually we see only one side, the side with all the promises. The back of the sign tells us their true destination: sorrow and sickness of body, mind, and spirit.

Nobody is obliged to pick up these passengers. No matter what our conditioning, each of us has the freedom to drive past without even giving negative thoughts a glance. If we do not stop and let them in, they cannot go anywhere; because they are not real until we support them. There is sympathy in the world: pick it up. There is antipathy in the world: don't pick it up. Hatred destroys. Love heals.

*It is here, my daughters, that love is to be
found – not hidden away in corners but in
the midst of occasions of sin. And believe
me, although we may more often fail
and commit small lapses, our gain will
be incomparably the greater.*

SAINT TERESA OF AVILA

The widest possibilities for spiritual growth lie
in the give-and-take of everyday relationships.
The truth of this is brought out sweetly in a story
about Saint Francis of Assisi. Three young men
approached Francis and asked his blessing to become hermits and seek God – each in his own
cave, deep in the mountains of Umbria. Francis
smiled. He instructed them to be hermits indeed, but hermits all together in a single hut.
One should take the role of father; a second
should think of himself as the mother; and the
third should be their child. Every few months
they should exchange roles. Living in this way
they were to establish among themselves perfect
harmony, thinking always of the needs of one
another.

We can almost see the three would-be recluses
exchanging sidelong glances. Their teacher had
issued them a greater challenge than any they
had bargained for. Yet they carried out Francis's
instructions, discovering that human relationships are the perfect tool for sanding away our
rough edges and getting at the core of divinity
within us. We need look no further than our own
family, friends, acquaintances, or even adver-
saries, to begin our practice.

Love seeks no cause beyond itself and no
fruit; it is its own fruit, its own enjoyment.
I love because I love; I love in order
that I may love.

SAINT BERNARD

It takes a lot of experience of life to see why some relationships last and others do not. But we do not have to wait for a crisis to get an idea of the future of a particular relationship. Our behavior in little everyday incidents tells us a great deal.

We only need to ask ourselves, "Am I ready to put the other person first?" If the answer is yes, that relationship is likely to grow deeper and more rewarding with the passage of time, whatever problems may come. If the answer is no, that relationship may not be able to withstand the testing that life is bound to bring. Sooner or later self-will is going to rebel when things don't go its way, and whoever happens to be closest will likely bear the brunt of it.

Relationships break down not because people are bad but because they are illiterate in love. To become literate in love, we must learn how to reduce our lifelong preoccupation with our own needs and feelings.

All that we are
is the result of what we have thought.

THE BUDDHA

The Buddha is saying that we made the circumstances we find ourselves in today. We got ourselves into them by all the deep-seated ways of thinking that led us into the actions, plans, behavior, and situations whose sum total is our lives.

But our destiny is in our own hands. Since we are formed by our thoughts, it follows that what we shall be tomorrow is shaped by what we think today.

Happily, we can choose the way we think. We can choose our feelings, aspirations, desires, and the way we view our world and ourselves. Mastery of the mind opens avenues of hope. We can begin to reshape our life and character, rebuild relationships, thrive in the stress of daily living, become the kind of person we want to be.

This is the true joy in life,
the being used for a purpose recognized
by yourself as a mighty one.
GEORGE BERNARD SHAW

All of us have tasted the freedom and happiness that self-forgetfulness brings. In watching a good game of tennis or becoming engrossed in a novel, the satisfaction comes not so much from what we are watching or reading as from the act of absorption itself. For that brief span, our burden of personal thoughts is forgotten; then we find relief, for what lies beneath that burden is the still, clear state of awareness we call joy.

The scientist or the artist absorbed in creative work is happy because she has forgotten herself in what she is doing. But nowhere will you find personalities so joyous, so unabashedly light-hearted, as those who have lost themselves in love for all. That is the joy we glimpse in Saint Francis, or Mira Bai, or Mahatma Gandhi. To look at the lives of men and women like these is to see what joy means.

As irrigators lead water where they want,
as archers make their arrows straight,
as carpenters carve wood,
the wise shape their minds.

THE BUDDHA

The Compassionate Buddha sums up the spiritual life in one simple phrase: "going against the current" – the current of all our conditioning, in how we act, how we speak, and even how we think.

Imagine swimming in a river flowing swiftly after monsoon rains – not floating downstream with the current, but swimming straight across, not letting the current sweep you from your course. That is the kind of spirit you need for meditation. When a flood of anger is sweeping over you with monsoon swiftness, that's no time to let yourself be carried away. Swim against it; that's what it means to live. You will feel your arms almost breaking, your endurance stretched to the limit, but you'll discover there is such satisfaction in the achievement that nothing easier will seem worthy of your effort again.

That is why the spiritual life appeals to the adventurous. It is only when you take on this challenge that you begin to understand the daring and the resolute, dauntless spirit it requires.

*When one is rising, standing, walking, doing
something, stopping, one should constantly
concentrate one's mind on the act and the
doing of it, not on one's relation to the act, or
its character or value. . . . One should simply
practice concentration of the mind on the act
itself, understanding it to be an expedient
means for attaining tranquillity of mind,
realization, insight and wisdom.*

ASHVAGHOSHA

Meditation is a dynamic discipline for learning
to focus our complete concentration at will. We
can practice this one-pointedness throughout
the day by doing one thing at a time, and giving
our full attention to whatever we are doing.

While having breakfast, for example, we can
give our complete attention to the food and not
to the newspaper. If we are listening to a friend,
even if a parrot flies down and perches on his
head, we should not get excited, point to the parrot, and burst out, "Excuse me for interrupting,
but there's a parrot on your head." We should be
able to concentrate so hard on what our friend is
saying that we can tell this urge, "Keep quiet and
don't distract me. Afterwards, I'll tell him about
the bird."

There is a close connection between deep
concentration and love, and with the practice of
one-pointed attention we can greatly increase
the precious capacity to remain loving and loyal
no matter what the vicissitudes or circumstances
we encounter.

The mantram becomes one's staff of life,
and carries one through every ordeal. It is
no empty repetition. For each repetition
has a new meaning, carrying you
nearer and nearer to God.

MAHATMA GANDHI

The mantram is the living symbol of the profoundest ideal that the human being can conceive of, the highest that we can respond to and love. When we repeat the mantram in our mind, we are reminding ourselves of the supreme Reality enshrined in our hearts. The more we repeat the mantram, the deeper it sinks into our consciousness. As it begins to connect with this Reality, it strengthens our will, heals old sources of conflict and turmoil, and gives us access to deeper sources of strength, patience, and love.

He that loveth not,
knoweth not God, for God is love.
I JOHN

These words sound so ethereal that most of us cannot connect them with daily life. What, we ask, do personal relationships have to do with the divine? I would reply that it is by discovering the unity between ourselves and others – *all* others – that we find our unity with God. We don't first get to know God and then, by some miracle of grace, come to love our fellow human beings. Loving others comes first: learning to love is how we move closer to the Lord. In this sense, learning to love is practicing religion. Those who can put the welfare of others before their own small personal interests are religious, even if they would deny it.

*Put your heart, mind, intellect, and
soul even to your smallest acts.
This is the secret of success.*

SWAMI SIVANANDA

One of the practical reasons for meditating is to
tap its power to solve problems that come up
throughout the day. It is very much like getting
momentum in a track event. While watching the
Olympics on television for the first time, I was
surprised to see how far back some of the ath-
letes went to get a running start. In the pole vault
one chap walked up to the bar, then turned
around and strode so far back that I thought he
had decided to go home. If you didn't know
about the pole vault you might think, "What's
the matter with this fellow? Instead of compet-
ing, he's running away."

He's not running away; he's going back to get
the momentum he needs for a really big jump.
That is the purpose of meditation, too. Instead
of getting out of bed and plunging directly into
life's maelstrom unprepared, you sit down for a
half hour in meditation to get a good start. Then
when you go out into the world, you have a good
reserve of energy and security on which to draw.

Love bears it out even to the edge of doom.
WILLIAM SHAKESPEARE

Most of us spend years in personal pursuits without ever taking time to know the needs of people in our own home, in our neighborhood, at work. It may be rarely that we give our energy to serving their needs. We sometimes forget that our nascent capacity for love is the greatest thing we shall ever have. To nurture it, we should subordinate everything else. That means we may have to forget our private adventures in profit and pleasure for the sake of others, but that is how love grows.

It takes a lifetime to learn to love. Love does not burst forth one morning with a display of fireworks in the depths of meditation. It grows little by little every day, by bearing with people, as Shakespeare's sonnet says, "even to the edge of doom." That is what love requires. But if we make it our number one priority, no matter what difficulties come our way, our love cannot help but grow.

*You learn to speak by speaking, to study
by studying, to run by running, to work
by working; in just the same way,
you learn to love by loving.*

SAINT FRANCIS DE SALES

Love grows by practice; there is no other way. Whenever you forgo something you want to do in order to give your time and help to those around you, you are increasing your capacity to love.

Naturally, at the beginning there will be reservations: "All right, we'll go to the opera, but I still prefer *Conan the Barbarian*!" That is the time to ignore your reservations, put on a smile, and repeat the mantram. As you begin to forget yourself and see how much your friend is enjoying the opera, or how much your little girl is enjoying her fourth performance of *Alice in Wonderland*, your reservations will fade away. By putting the people around you first, you *are* loving more, not only them but the Lord himself, in whom they and you are one.

*We have to take the whole universe as
the expression of the one Self. Then only
our love flows to all beings and creatures
in the world equally.*

SWAMI RAMDAS

You and I appear to be separate. We differ in color, size, and shape. Differences in ideas, tastes, and prejudices mark us as individuals to be reckoned with. Beneath this apparent division, however, lies hidden deep within each of us the one Self – eternal, infinite, ever-perfect. This is the closely guarded secret of life: that we are all caught up in a divine masquerade, and all we are trying to do is take off our masks to reveal the pure, perfect Self within.

In our present condition, we have forgotten we are wearing masks. Fortunately, the Lord will not allow us to forget him, but keeps on calling us to him. In order to find him, we must look deep within ourselves through the practice of meditation. When we succeed, our purpose in life will be fulfilled, and all our anger against others will melt into unfathomable love, all our fear of others into unshakable security. The great mystics of all religions refer to this state as union with the Lord.

Love is patient and kind; love is not jealous
or boastful; it is not arrogant or rude.

I CORINTHIANS

To excel in anything you have to have patience;
but if you want to love, patience is an absolute
necessity. You may be dashing, glamorous, fascinating, and alluring; you may be tall, dark, and
handsome; or lissome and blond; or whatever
the current fancy may be. Without patience,
you can never become a great lover; it would be
a contradiction in terms.

"Well," most of us say, "I guess that leaves me
out. Patience has never been my strong suit."
Very, very few of us are born patient. Our age
has been called the age of anxiety, the age of
anger; but we could just as easily say the age of
impatience. You see it in supermarket lines, on
the highway, on the tennis court, in the school-
yard, in the political arena, on the bus. With all
this we have begun to believe that impatience is
our natural state. Fortunately, love is our natural state, and patience is something that everybody can learn.

*Just as a fire is covered by smoke and a
mirror is obscured by dust, just as the
embryo rests deep within the womb,
wisdom is hidden by selfish desire.*

SRI KRISHNA (BHAGAVAD GITA)

This verse is taken from the Bhagavad Gita, a short Sanskrit work of seven hundred verses that has fascinated and inspired mystics, physicists, psychologists, and philosophers of many countries for three thousand years. Set on a battlefield on the morning before a fierce battle, the Gita uses warfare as a metaphor for our personal battle with the challenges of life.

The Gita's message is simple but profound: our native state is freedom. What we want most from life is to be free of all the mental compulsions that keep us from living in peace with ourselves, with others, and with the environment. This desire for freedom is at the core of our personality, says the Gita, and our failings – whether they be insensitivity to the suffering of others, or greed, or anger, or fear – only hide our real nature like dust obscuring the face of a mirror.

*They live in wisdom who see themselves
in all and all in them, who have renounced
every selfish desire and sense craving
tormenting the heart.*

SRI KRISHNA (BHAGAVAD GITA)

The Gita's hypothesis is that it is possible, by mastering the thinking process, to leave behind unwanted habits and negative thoughts. To accomplish this, the Gita outlines a daily course of training in which we acquire conscious control of our attention, strengthening our will at such a deep level of the unconscious that no compulsive desire or addiction can sweep us away. What is the predicted result? When your will is linked to your intellect at the very depths of your personality, you discover yourself as you really are – secure, wise, compassionate, and intimately connected with all of life.

This training is available to all. It requires no special equipment, no expensive outlay of cash. All that is needed is desire . . . and daring.

Be strong and of a good courage, fear not,
nor be afraid . . . for the Lord thy God,
he it is that doth go with thee;
he will not fail thee, nor forsake thee.

DEUTERONOMY

Whenever we worry about something in the past or the future, we are setting up our own little haunted house and peopling it with our own special ghosts.

Many years ago I stayed at the home of an hospitable woman who happened to believe in ghosts. Her home had a beautiful view which took in a cemetery nearby, and though she was very fond of me, nothing I could say could convince her that ghosts from that cemetery did not pay her visits. So one day I announced casually that I was going for a walk in the cemetery.

When I returned she was wringing her hands. "Did you see any ghosts?" she asked anxiously.

"Oh, yes," I said. "Three. I told them you were too nice a woman to be living in fear all the time, and they should go away and leave you alone."

"And what did they say?" she giggled.

"They said, 'We can't. As long as she believes in us, we *have* to stay.'"

She stared at me for a second, then laughed out loud. Those ghosts never bothered her again.

*Love the whole world as a mother
loves her only child.*

THE BUDDHA

When you discover the divine core of your personality – call it Christ, or the Buddha, or
Krishna, the Divine Mother, or simply the
Infinite – you are not just transformed; you are
transfigured. You are no longer in love merely
with persons A, B, and C; you become love itself. You live in the City of Love.

Every person on the face of the earth moves
you to love. It is not possible for you to think ill
of anybody or to hurt anybody. You strive to
live your life in a manner that never infringes on
the happiness of anyone. You make a contribution to solving the immense problems that
trouble people today.

You are quaffing drink from a hundred
fountains: whenever any of these hundred
yields less, your pleasure is diminished.
But when the sublime fountain gushes from
within you, no longer need you steal from
the other fountains.

JALALUDDIN RUMI

Often, we are most vulnerable during moments of transition. For example, you have wrapped up one assignment, and it is time to look over the next. Or you've turned the last page of your novel, and it is time to go to bed. Whatever the transition, for a pivotal moment the mind has nothing to hold on to, and in its insecurity it may suggest all kinds of things: a cigarette, an extra piece of pie, a magazine promising the lowdown on your favorite actor's private life. Suddenly any of these can seem fraught with urgency, though you know in the back of your mind that they are a poor use of your time.

Here the mantram can rescue you. If you start repeating the Holy Name the moment you complete one activity, and do not drop it until the time comes for you to give complete attention to the next job at hand, your will gets a needed boost. A short, fast walk repeating the mantram can be more refreshing than all manner of "treats." Once you are absorbed again, you are home free.

*Dreams are real as long as they last.
Can we say more of life?*
HENRY HAVELOCK ELLIS

When we wake up from a dream, the mystics say, we do not pass from unreality to reality; we pass from a lower level of reality to a higher level. And, they add, there is a higher level still, compared with which this waking life of ours is as insubstantial as a dream. To put it rather bluntly, we are living in our sleep, dreaming that things like money and pleasure can make us happy. When they do not, it's a nightmare.

Yet until we do wake up, nothing sounds more absurd than the assertion that we are dreaming – and nothing seems more solid than this world of the senses. Why should this be so? If original goodness is our real nature, why are we unable to see it? The mystics' answer is simple: because we see life not as it is but as we are. We see "through a glass darkly," through the distorting lenses of the mind – all the layers of feeling, habit, instinct, and memory that cover the pure core of goodness deep within.

On this path, effort never goes to waste,
and there is no failure. Even a little effort
toward spiritual awareness will protect
you from the greatest fear.

SRI KRISHNA (BHAGAVAD GITA)

The smallest effort is not lost,
Each wavelet on the ocean tost
Aids in the ebb-tide or the flow;
Each rain-drop makes some floweret blow;
Each struggle lessens human woe.

CHARLES MACKAY

On the spiritual path, no effort goes to waste. Even if we meditate only thirty minutes every morning, and try to practice the allied spiritual disciplines to a small extent during the day, this can go a long way in guarding us against many dangers, known and unknown. To be truly secure, we must begin to find a source of security within ourselves.

We must make every effort to move forward even if it is little by little, even if every day we keep making mistakes. Sometimes we are so insensitive and preoccupied with ourselves that when we try to put others first we simply are not aware of their needs. Our mistakes begin to haunt us; but rather than sitting in a corner and crying over the day's errors, or developing a guilt complex, we should repeat the mantram and make sure that we do not repeat the same mistakes the next day.

*All spiritual disciplines are done with
a view to still the mind. The perfectly
still mind is universal spirit.*

SWAMI RAMDAS

Meditation is the regular, systematic training of attention to turn inward and dwell continuously on a single focus within consciousness. After many years of practice, we can become so absorbed in the object of our contemplation that while we are meditating, we forget ourselves completely. In that moment, when we may be said to be empty of ourselves, we are utterly full of what we are dwelling on. This is the central principle of meditation: we become what we meditate on.

Eventually, meditation will make our mind calm, clear, and as concentrated as a laser – which we can focus at will. This capacity of one-pointed attention is the essence of genius. When we have this mastery over attention in everything we do, we have a genius for life itself: unshakable security, clear judgment, and deep personal relationships.

*A devotee who can call on God while
living a householder's life is a hero indeed.
God thinks: "He is blessed indeed who prays
to Me in the midst of his worldly duties. He
is trying to find Me, overcoming a great
obstacle – pushing away, as it were, a
huge block of stone weighing a ton.
Such a man is a real hero."*

SRI RAMAKRISHNA

To lead the spiritual life, it is not necessary to give up our job, leave our family, change our religion, or travel to distant lands. We start wherever we are, not running away from society, but right in the midst of life.

Whatever context we find ourselves in is a suitable one in which to overcome our problems and grow to our full height. We tend to look upon the *other* home as peaceful, the other couple as perfect, the other parent-child relationship as ideal, but this is not very likely. Everyone has certain liabilities as well as assets. Everyone has done some good, and made some mistakes as well. This is part of the human condition.

The mystics are loving realists. "Don't wait for ideal conditions. You'll never find them," they admonish. "Begin! And the conditions you need will come to you."

Let sleep itself be an exercise in piety,
for such as our life and conduct have been,
so also of necessity will be our dreams.

SAINT BASIL

One of the best times to repeat the mantram is while falling asleep at night. Tuck yourself in, close your eyes, and start repeating your mantram until you fall asleep in it.

Other thoughts may try to push the mantram away. But through sheer persistence you can achieve a minor miracle. Between the last waking moment and the first sleeping moment, there is an arrow's entry into deepest consciousness. If you can send your mantram in through that narrow gate, it will go on repeating itself in your sleep, healing old wounds and restoring your peace of mind for the next day.

The Lord is quite happy to work all night. Those who have learned to fall asleep in the Holy Name go forward even in their sleep.

*For the outer sense alone perceives
visible things and the eye of the heart alone,
sees the invisible.*

RICHARD OF SAINT-VICTOR

*I found Thee not, O Lord, without,
because I erred in seeking Thee without
that were within.*

SAINT AUGUSTINE

The senses are the servants of consciousness. If they are unruly – clamoring for what is not exactly healthy – it is just because they've been badly raised. They are unschooled. "Why do you behave so terribly?" we ask in exasperation. "We can't help it," is all they can say.

The senses are used to being stimulated all the time. Every billboard screams that satisfaction lies outside – that we will experience joy if we will only taste this pizza or drink that wine, listen to this music or see that movie. No wonder we get caught in the idea that happiness lies in indulging the senses and that a lot of vital energy is trapped in living out this belief.

After many years of training my discrimination to be their benevolent boss, my senses never let me down. They might clamor briefly for the chocolate mousse on the pastry cart, but a firm "Careful!" brings them right back to the fresh strawberries. I have their complete, joyful cooperation now – but the victory hasn't come easily.

*Time is what keeps the light from reaching
us. There is no greater obstacle to God than
time: and not only time but temporalities,
not only temporal things but temporal
affections, not only temporal affections
but the very taint and smell of time.*

MEISTER ECKHART

We think that past and future are real because
the mind keeps brooding over what we have
done and what others have done to us, what we
will do and what others will do to us. But it is not
past and future that are real; it is our brooding on
the past and the future that is real. If we could
withdraw our attention from these will-o'-the-
wisps, many of our problems would simply dissolve.

As our meditation deepens, we develop the
ability to withdraw our attention more and
more from the past and the future to focus it on
the present. And as we begin to live more and
more in the present, we make the exhilarating
discovery that past and future exist only in our
minds. It is a tremendous realization, for it
means that we are released from any burden of
guilt about the past and any anxiety about the future.

Every moment is unique and discrete. When
our concentration is complete, we rest completely in the present. Then we do not live in
time, we live in eternity.

No man is an island, entire of itself;
every man is a piece of the continent,
a part of the main.

JOHN DONNE

The unity underlying life is so complete and pervasive that when we inflict suffering on the smallest creature, we injure the whole. When we refrain from habits that harm others, when we take up jobs that relieve suffering, when we work to put an end to anger and separateness, we strengthen the whole.

There is nothing more important in life than learning to express this unity in all our relationships. Violence, war, and insensitivity to our fellow creatures are external manifestations of the disunity seething in our consciousness. When we begin to practice spiritual disciplines, right from the first day, however slowly, we begin to transform our character, conduct, and consciousness. When the divisiveness which has been agitating us and making life difficult begins to mend, we get immediate evidence in our daily life. Our health improves, long-standing personal conflicts subside, our mind becomes clearer, and a sense of security and well-being follows us wherever we go.

*Better indeed is knowledge than
mechanical practice. Better than knowledge
is meditation. But better still is surrender
of attachment to results, because
there follows immediate peace.*

SRI KRISHNA (BHAGAVAD GITA)

When it comes to something as important as
Self-realization, I am the kind of person who
won't leave any stone unturned. Even if it is only
a little pebble, I have to turn it over. If I am going
to devote so many years of my life to extinguishing the ego, I want to make sure it is extinguished
once and for all.

So even if Sri Krishna himself were to assure
me that meditation is enough by itself, I would
still say, "Excuse me, Lord. It may be enough
for the Compassionate Buddha, but a little person like me can't afford to take chances. I'm
going to do everything I possibly can: meditate
and put others first *and* learn to be detached
from the results of action, all together." It is a
very practical attitude, which I must have absorbed from my grandmother's example: there
is always something more that you can do.

*Everybody today seems to be in such
a terrible rush, anxious for greater
developments and greater riches and so on,
so that children have very little time for their
parents. Parents have very little time for
each other, and in the home begins the
disruption of the peace of the world.*

MOTHER TERESA OF CALCUTTA

In going faster and faster, and trying our hand at new adventures all the time, we hope we can forget our emptiness. We try to squeeze as many jobs as possible into a limited span of time. We're in some frantic race, not knowing just why or against whom we're racing.

There is no joy in work which is hurried, which is done when we are at the mercy of pressures from outside, because such work is compulsive. All too often hurry clouds judgment. More and more, to save time, a person tends to think in terms of pat solutions and to take short-cuts and give uninspired performances.

It is often said that life in our modern world is so complicated, so busy, and so crowded that just to survive we have to hurry. But I think we still have a choice. We can insist on working conditions that do not force us to hurry. It is possible to do our work and attend to our duties without being oppressed by time, and when we work free from the bondage of time we do not make mistakes, we do not get tense, and the quality of our living improves.

And God shall wipe away all tears from
their eyes; and there shall be no more death,
neither sorrow, nor crying, neither shall
there be any more pain.

REVELATION

We have all seen those signs on the highway, "Go Back. Wrong Way!" Where roads are concerned, we all understand this warning. We turn around. If only we could understand life's signs so easily!

Sorrow is often a warning with the same message: "Go back. Change your direction. You are going the wrong way." Every creature is conditioned to avoid pain; this is a built-in safety mechanism to protect our bodies from harm. When you eat more than necessary, for example, you should feel reassured if your stomach aches. Your body is telling you, "Please don't do this again; it's not good for me." Mental and emotional suffering often serve the same function.

Once we have connected our sorrow with particular patterns of behavior, we will remember to act wisely more often. Eventually, when all its lessons have been learned, personal sorrow will vanish from our life altogether.

All mystics speak the same language,
for they come from the same country.

LOUIS-CLAUDE DE SAINT-MARTIN

What we are all looking for, even though we are searching in the most improbable places, is infinite wisdom, infinite joy, infinite love. In other words, we are trying to discover our real nature. At the very core of our being is a spark of purity, of perfection, of divinity. When we learn to identify less and less with that which is subject to change and more and more with this core of perfection, we are gradually moving closer to this supreme goal.

Though different religions call it by different names, the goal is always the same. It is *nirvana* to the Buddhist, *moksha* to the Hindu; Jesus calls it "entering the kingdom of heaven within." To the Sufis it is union with the Beloved; to Jewish mystics it is the return to the Promised Land. No matter what they call it, all the great religions point to the same supreme goal.

Pilgrimage to the place of the wise is to find escape from the flame of separateness.

JALALUDDIN RUMI

Self-will is love turned around. Love is energy, and self-will is that energy focused on itself. We can learn to free that energy, and when we do, our lives will fill up with love, which is what living in heaven means.

To live as a separate creature, cut off from the rest of life, is just the opposite of joy. Self-will hardens into a solid wall that keeps others out and ourselves walled in. When we feel intense anguish in a personal relationship, more often than not what pains us is self-will, aching because it cannot have its way.

Nirvana – *nir*, 'out,' *vana*, 'to blow,' – is the Compassionate Buddha's term for the process of blowing out self-will, which enables us bit by bit to realize the indivisible unity of life. When we extinguish self-will, anguish turns into joy and wisdom.

Among the attributes of God, although they are all equal, mercy shines with even more brilliancy than justice.

MIGUEL DE CERVANTES

In Kerala, the state in South India from which I come, along the roadside there are stone parapets the height of a person's head. When people need to rest from carrying heavy loads of rice or fruit on their heads, they stand next to the parapet and shift their load onto it.

The Lord is the perennial parapet, standing at exactly the right height for each one of us. For those who are very selfish, he stands very tall to support an awesome load; for those who are average in selfishness, he stands about six feet high; and for the selfless, the parapet can hardly be seen because the burden is so light that almost no support is needed. Through the practice of meditation, we can gradually learn to shift our load into the Lord's mighty arms.

We like to think that we make big decisions and carry terrible responsibilities on our shoulders. Our shoulders are bent, our back gives us problems, and we are too tired to stand on our feet because of the mighty burdens we try to bear. Few of us realize there is somebody standing with arms outstretched, just waiting to carry our burdens.

To be a Sufi is to cease from taking trouble;
and there is no greater trouble for thee than
thine own self, for when thou art occupied
with thyself, thou remainest away from God.

ABU SA'ID

Do you want to be free? Most of us are held hostage in life by our likes and dislikes. We are bound hand and foot by countless little preferences in food, clothing, decor, entertainment – the list goes on and on.

For example, the person with rigid tastes in food is likely to have rigid tastes elsewhere as well. He will probably enjoy only one kind of music, she will appreciate only one style of art, and when it comes to people, he has very definite allergies. In any case, he is conditioned to be happy only so long as he gets everything the way he likes it. Otherwise – which may be ninety-nine percent of the time – he is unhappy over something.

The way we respond to small matters reflects the way we will respond to the larger matters of life. So, if we can begin to release ourselves from our little likes and dislikes, we will find that we are gaining the capacity to weather emotional storms. Then we can try to face whatever comes calmly and courageously.

The enemy is more easily overcome
if he be not suffered to enter the door
of our hearts, but be resisted without
the gate at his first knock.

THOMAS A KEMPIS

The body is rather like a city with five gates, the five senses. We are fairly fussy about what enters the gate of the mouth. But just as food enters the mouth and goes on to nourish or damage the body, sense impressions enter consciousness through our eyes, ears, nose, and skin, and in most of us the traffic is somewhat unregulated. We all want to be open to experience, but we also need to be watchful. When impressions come knocking, we need to check IDs.

Take popular films, most of which glamorize violence. We can pretend this is only entertainment, bearing no relationship to real life, yet every year violent crimes enact with terrible precision episodes from television or movies. In our violent society, how can anyone argue convincingly that witnessing casual cruelty on television does not affect us? We all have a personal stake in not supporting any of the mass media when they give us poisonous food for our eyes, our ears, and our minds.

You are what your deep, driving desire is.

BRIHADARANYAKA UPANISHAD

Desire is the key to life, because desire is power. The deeper the desire, the more power it contains.

Most people start life with many small desires. Their power and vitality trickle away in many different directions. None of their desires is deep enough to contain much power. But there are people whose lives are molded by only a few, consuming desires. Such people usually achieve their goals. Because their desires are unified, their will becomes nearly invincible. To desire something deeply *is* to will it, and to will is to achieve. If they want to become a great artist, build a bigger pyramid, explain the movements of the planets, they devote their life to that, and usually succeed. Wherever you find great success in life, it is fueled by the intense unification of desires.

But the most successful people of all are the rare men and women like Mahatma Gandhi and Saint Teresa of Avila, who have but *one* desire. All lesser desires have been consumed in the great fire of love for God.

Nothing great was ever achieved
without enthusiasm.

RALPH WALDO EMERSON

We can do anything we want to do
if we stick to it long enough.

HELEN KELLER

Many people read about mysticism; many attend lectures on meditation; but few have the daring to meditate. It is hard work. To continue to practice it day in and day out requires real depth of desire and commitment.

This should not be surprising. After all, to attain excellence in anything we have to work at it. An Olympic swimming champion doesn't go for her workout once a week on Sunday afternoon; she swims for hours every day. The outstanding tennis player thinks tennis, eats tennis, and dreams tennis. The members of his family never worry about him, because they always know where to find him – on the tennis court.

Whether it is in tennis, or swimming, or meditation, mastery does not come from dabbling. We have to be prepared to pay the price. We need to have the sustained enthusiasm that motivates us to give our best. The more we give to our meditation, the more it gives to us.

If God gave the soul his whole creation
she would not be filled thereby
but only with himself.

MEISTER ECKHART

Today, even in a modern industrial society like the United States, we are not always able to provide food and shelter for all of our people. These are very real and important needs. But there are other needs that sometimes are not so easily identified. Even when the most pressing requirements for food or clothing or shelter have been satisfied, that is not enough for the human being. There remains a hunger for something more. We want to *be* somebody. We want to feel secure. We want to love. Without any better way to satisfy these inner needs, we end up depending on possessions and profit – not just for our physical well-being but as a substitute for the dignity, fulfillment, and security we want so much.

Only by living for something that lasts, something real – rather than for passing pleasure and profit – can we achieve the lasting fulfillment, the limitless capacity to love, that is our birthright.

As Plato sometimes speaks of the divine love,
it arises not out of indigency, as created love
does, but out of fullness and redundancy; it is
an overflowing fountain, and that love
which descends upon created being is a free
efflux from the almighty source of love: and
it is well pleasing to him that those creatures
which he hath made should partake of it.

JOHN SMITH THE PLATONIST

In India, where families often make severe sacrifices to send a son or daughter to college, everyone is patient with a student who is out of cash. If you are waiting in line for tickets with two or three friends, for example, and your turn comes at the box office window, everyone understands if you suddenly discover that your shoelace has come loose. You bend down to tie it, giving your friends a chance to buy your ticket, and everybody knows there is no question of generosity or stinginess; you simply do not have the capacity to pay.

Similarly, when someone suddenly gets angry, you can think to yourself, "Well, his shoelace has just come untied." He has just run out of inner resources. Whatever he was doing before, he has to bend down and look at his feet; he hasn't got attention to give to anything else. To grow rich in love – to make yourself into a real tycoon of tenderness – have patience with others.

*I claim to be an average man of less than
average ability. I have not the shadow
of a doubt that any man or woman
can achieve what I have, if he or she
would make the same effort and
cultivate the same hope and faith.*

MAHATMA GANDHI

While most people think of ordinariness as a fault or limitation, Gandhi had discovered in it the very meaning of life – and of history. For him, it was not the famous or the rich or the powerful who would change the course of history. If the future is to differ from the past, he taught, if we are to leave a peaceful and healthy earth for our children, it will be the ordinary man and woman who do it: not by becoming extraordinary, but by discovering that our greatest strength lies not in how much we differ from each other but in how much – how very much – we are the same.

This faith in the power of the individual formed the foundation for Gandhi's extremely compassionate view of the industrial era's large-scale problems, as well as of the smaller but no less urgent troubles we find in our own lives. One person *can* make a difference.

*Do not let your peace depend on the hearts
of men; whatever they say about you, good
or bad, you are not because of it another
man, for as you are, you are.*

THOMAS A KEMPIS

Even if you have ninety-nine persons cheering
you, there will always be a hundredth to boo.
That is the nature of life, and to deal with it, we
need simply to learn not always to be on the
lookout for appreciation and applause. If people
say, "Oh, there is nobody like you," don't get
elated. Don't go pick up your telephone and call
your friends to tell them what is being broadcast
about you. That's what most of us do, you
know; that's why telephones are so busy. It is
also why so many people are constantly getting
depressed when fortune seems to frown.

My spiritual teacher – a simple, straightforward woman who didn't mince words – used to
tell me, "You can't shut other people's mouths."
It took me years to understand that. This unlet-
tered lady knew that we don't have any control
over other people's minds. You can control only
your own mind. When you understand this,
you know you needn't be concerned about what
people say about you: it doesn't affect you, because your mind cannot be upset. You may feel
hurt, but you will have an inner security that
cannot be shaken.

Peace is not the absence of war,
it is a virtue, a state of mind,
a disposition for benevolence,
confidence, and justice.

SPINOZA

He insulted me, he cheated me, he beat me,
he robbed me – those who are free of
resentful thoughts surely find peace.

THE BUDDHA

Resentment is nothing more than compulsive attachment to a set of memories. If you could peek through the window of the mind when you feel resentful, you would see a production line turning out the same emotion-charged memory over and over: "He did that to me in 1983, he did that to me in 1983. . . ." You are dwelling on something that took place in the past – or, more likely, on how you misunderstood that event and reacted to your misunderstanding.

When you keep pumping attention into an event in this way, a limp little memory gets blown up into a big balloon of hostility. When you withdraw your attention by repeating the mantram, the balloon is deflated. It's as simple as that.

I tell you one thing – if you want peace of
mind, do not find fault with others.
Rather learn to see your own faults.
Learn to make the whole world your own.
No one is a stranger, my child;
this whole world is your own.

SRI SARADA DEVI

When we get even the slightest glimpse of the unity of life, we realize that in tearing others down we are tearing ourselves down too. When you sit in judgment on other people and countries and races, you're training your mind to sit in judgment on yourself. As we forgive others, we are teaching the mind to respond with forgiveness everywhere, even to the misdeeds and mistakes of our own past.

*The secret of health for both mind
and body is not to mourn for the past,
not to worry about the future,
or not to anticipate troubles,
but to live the present moment
wisely and earnestly.*

THE BUDDHA

When the mind is stilled through the practice of meditation, we are lifted out of time into the eternal present. The body, of course, is still subject to the passage of time. But in a sense, the flickering of the mind is our internal clock. When the mind does not flicker, what is there to measure change? Time simply comes to a stop for us – or, more accurately, we live completely in the present moment. Past and future, after all, exist only in the mind. When the mind stops, there is no past or future. We cannot be resentful, we cannot be guilt-ridden, we cannot build future hopes and desires and fears on past experiences; no energy flows to past or future at all.

Past and future are both contained in every present moment. Whatever we are today is the result of what we have thought, spoken, and done in all the present moments before now – just as what we shall be tomorrow is the result of what we think, say, and do today. The responsibility for both present and future is in our own hands. If we live right today, then tomorrow has to be right.

*This life of separateness may be compared
to a dream, a phantasm, a bubble, a shadow,
a drop of dew, a flash of lightning.*

THE BUDDHA

Time runs out so soon! In our teens and twenties, even our thirties, we have ample margin to play with the toys life has to offer. But we should find out soon how fleeting they are, for the tides of time can ebb away before we know it. We live from moment to moment by God's grace, and none of us knows when Death will come to cut the thread of our lives.

Time *is* death. As we grow older and our family and friends begin to pass away, we see how relentlessly time is pursuing all of us; every death should remind us of the imminence of our own. There is no time to quarrel, no time to feel resentful or estranged. There is no time to waste on the pursuit of selfish pleasures that are over almost before they begin.

The all-devouring jaws of time are following us always, closer than our shadow. As long as I live only for myself, as a feverish little fragment apart from the whole, I cannot escape the jaws of time. It is good to bear in mind how evanescent life is so that we do not postpone the voyage across this sea of separate existence, the ceaseless process of birth and death.

*The control of the palate is a valuable aid
for the control of the mind.*

MAHATMA GANDHI

I first became interested in improving my diet under the influence of Mahatma Gandhi, who used to include articles on diet and health in his weekly newspaper, along with all the latest political news. I had been brought up on traditional South Indian cuisine. I had enjoyed it all thoroughly, but I had never asked what the purpose of food is. At Gandhi's prompting, I started asking this kind of question and concluded to my great surprise that food is meant to nourish the body.

I started changing. I began to eat foods that wouldn't have appealed to me in earlier days. Now asparagus tastes better than chocolate torte.

The palate is the ideal starting point for getting some mastery over your senses. You have three, four, maybe more opportunities a day: breakfast, lunch, dinner, and any number of between-meal snacks. No need to talk of fasting, or strange diets. Just resolve to move away from foods that don't benefit your health and begin choosing foods that do. With this simple resolution, you'll strengthen your will, and deepen your meditation.

*The grace of God is a wind
which is always blowing.*

SRI RAMAKRISHNA

All that you and I have to do is to put up our sails
and let this wind carry us across the sea of life to
the other shore. But most of us are firmly stuck
on this shore. Our sail is in tatters and our boat
cannot move because of all the excess baggage
weighing it down: our likes and dislikes, our
habits and opinions, all the resentments and
hostilities which we have carefully acquired.

But just as it is we, ourselves, who have acquired this baggage, it is we who can gradually
learn to toss it overboard. The wind is blowing,
but we have to make our boat seaworthy. We can
patch up our sail, and unfurl it to catch the wind
that will carry us to the other shore.

*If you purify your soul of attachment to and
desire for things, you will understand them
spiritually. If you deny your appetite
for them, you will enjoy their truth,
understanding what is certain in them.*

SAINT JOHN OF THE CROSS

The mind should be a reliable instrument of observation, but it very often is not, because it is so deeply influenced by the compulsive habits and addictions that characterize so much of modern life. Comparing the mind to a camera, you could say that these habits skew the focus, alter the depth of field, and in general do all they can to make us see not what is really there but what the mind wants us to see. And what it wants us to see is the profit or momentary gratification it is interested in, whether it is a pastry or a sports car, a promotion or a dividend. When our attention is glued to these things, we see only the fragmented, turbulent surface of life, not the vast interconnected web of relationships supporting that surface.

Through meditation, we unglue the mind from the tantalizing surface, and make it turn inwards. Then we begin to see life in a completely new way – not as a struggle to get what we want no matter what the cost, but as a compassionate dance, where each creature has a beautiful role.

Purity of heart is to will one thing.
SOREN KIERKEGAARD

There is a Hindu story comparing the mind to the trunk of an elephant – restless, inquisitive, always straying. In our villages in India, elephants are sometimes taken in religious processions through the streets to the temple. The streets are crooked and narrow, lined on either side with fruit and vegetable stalls. Along comes the elephant with his restless trunk, and in one sinuous motion, it grabs a whole bunch of bananas. He opens his cavernous mouth, and tosses the bananas in – stalk and all. From the next stall he picks up a coconut and tosses it in after the bananas.

No threats or promises can make this restless trunk settle down. But the wise mahout will give that trunk a short bamboo stick to hold. Then the elephant will walk along proudly, holding the bamboo stick in front like a drum major with a baton. He doesn't steal bananas and coconuts now, because his trunk has something to hold on to.

The mind is the same way. We can keep it from straying into all kinds of situations if we just give it the mantram.

The body is mortal,
but he who dwells in the body
is immortal and immeasurable.

SRI KRISHNA (BHAGAVAD GITA)

When I say that this body is not me, I am not making an intellectual statement. It is an experiential statement. If you were to ask me, "Who is this body?" I would make an awful pun: "This is my buddy. I give him good food and good exercise, and I look after him very well, but he is not me."

My body has always been my faithful buddy, through many trials, and during many difficult times; and I let him know how much I appreciate his faithful service. We have an understanding: I take very good care of him, and he looks up to me as the boss.

As Saint Francis used to say, "This body is Brother Donkey. I feed him, I wash him, but *I* am going to ride on *him*."

Whenever we use drugs, or smoke, or drink, or even overeat, the donkey is riding on *us*. The mystics challenge us: "Don't you want to get that donkey off your back and ride on *it*?"

To display His eternal attributes
In their inexhaustible variety,
The Lord made the green fields
of time and space.

JAMI

The Lord has strewn little signs of his presence throughout the universe. The person who is observant will see these signs and know where the Lord is to be found. There is a marvelous story about a man looking for the Buddha the way one follows the tracks of an animal in the jungle. He went around talking to people everywhere, and whenever he found a person whose life had been transformed he would exclaim, "Those are the tracks of a really big elephant!"

The men and women who have realized God leave big, unmistakable tracks. In a smaller way, when we see someone being extremely patient, someone who can listen quietly to criticism without retaliating or losing her temper, we might think, "Aha! That's not my friend Jane, that is the Lord in Jane." Jane is leaving a trail – broken twigs of patience, torn leaves of kindness – all subtle signs by which we can track the Lord's presence.

Though the Lord is present everywhere, the expression of his presence varies throughout the infinite variety of his creation. Wherever perfection is approached, his glory is revealed a little more – among people, among trees, among mountains, among stars.

Thy desire is thy prayer; and if
thy desire is without ceasing, thy prayer
will also be without ceasing. . . .
The continuance of your longing
is the continuance of your prayer.

SAINT AUGUSTINE

I once had a physicist friend who would gladly discuss electric power; but harnessing the power of a passion or a craving – well, that was not dynamics; that was poetry. "Power," he told me sternly, "is the capacity to do work. Work is the energy required to move a definite mass a definite distance. No movement, no work. No work, no power."

Day or night I had never seen my friend far from his desk. Then late one evening I came out of a movie theater and saw him striding along like an athlete, several miles from his office. "What got you up from your desk?" I asked. "You're breaking the habits of a lifetime."

"Coffee," he muttered. "I ran out of coffee."

"Here," I said, "a very definite mass has been propelled at least three miles, simply by one little desire for a cup of coffee." He got my point.

Every deep desire is a prayer. Every desire also contains a certain quantum of energy – energy to grasp the desired goal.

Hatred does not cease through hatred
at any time. Hatred ceases through love.
This is an unalterable law.

THE BUDDHA

In order to work for peace, we should have an adequate sense of detachment from the results of our work. If we are going to get agitated every time there is a reversal, we ourselves will become violent. As we know, sometimes even demonstrators against violence become violent.

To paraphrase the wise words of the Buddha, "Violence will not cease by violence. Violence ceases by nonviolence. This is an unalterable law." In order to win over opposition, we have to be serene and compassionate. Most of us look upon defeat and reversals as weakening us; but in the spiritual life, when we are defeated it is possible to go deeper into our consciousness to bring out greater resources. Mahatma Gandhi was at his best when seemingly defeated. He used to say that he struck his hardest bargains from prison.

Defeat is found very often in the lives of selfless people as an opening into opportunity. When you follow the spiritual path, living for others, there come to you increased challenges, to make you go deeper and deeper into your consciousness. If there were no difficulties, you would only be skimming on the surface of life. Gandhi, in a rare statement in which he gave himself away, said, "I love storms."

*Indeed many things which we shall not
be able to discover either by the experiment
of work or by the investigations of reason,
we shall deserve to be taught by
importunate prayer, by the
revelation of divine inspiration.*

RICHARD OF SAINT-VICTOR

Usually it takes some time to find the right pace for meditation. For most of us the mind has been racing at top speed in overdrive for many years. In meditation we are slowing it down, gradually shifting into a lower and lower gear. But do not pace the words so slowly that you go into reverse.

When you can make your mind go through the passage at its slowest speed – which means you have really learned to concentrate – there is a living charge in the words. They fall deep into your consciousness and come to life. As you are repeating them their application to daily living comes right along with their meaning. At this time you are not just meditating on words. You are meditating on the vital applications of eternal truth to daily living. The proof will be that after you finish meditation, these applications will follow you through the day, to help you make wise choices in what to eat, how to work, how to give your best to your job and to those around you.

It is no little wisdom for a man to keep himself in silence and in good peace when evil words are spoken to him, and to turn his heart to God and not to be troubled with man's judgment.

THOMAS A KEMPIS

Most of us appreciate praise, but it is disastrous to become dependent on it. If we are going to allow our security to be bolstered up by the praise, appreciation, and applause of others, we are done for. I have heard about a well-known movie star who goes to sleep at night with a tape of recorded applause playing. This is going to make him more and more insecure.

Why should we get agitated if someone ignores us? There are, after all, advantages to being ignored. We can go anywhere in freedom. Nobody recognizes us – how good it is! In life, there are occasions when we are ignored and sometimes forgotten. That is the time for us to remind ourselves, "Why should I need anybody's attention?" This is the attitude of the real mystic, who is content because he or she is complete. This attitude can be cultivated skillfully.

Even those of us who are the most sensitive to praise and appreciation can learn to be so secure within ourselves that the word *rejected* can be expelled from our dictionary. The one person who will never reject us is the Lord within, and that is enough to make up for all the rejections we may have to undergo at the hands of everyone else.

God loveth a cheerful giver.
II CORINTHIANS

In India we have a story about a man who was the perfect model of respectability, who always did what the letter of the law demanded. When he died, he was taken before Chitragupta, the cosmic auditor. Chitragupta looked at the man's record. There was not a single entry on the debit page. Chitragupta was impressed. Then he turned to the credit page and stared in astonishment. This page, too, was completely blank. Chitragupta didn't know what to do. The man had never helped anybody, never hurt anybody, never offended anybody, never loved anybody. He couldn't be sent to heaven, but he couldn't be sent to hell, either.

So Chitragupta took him to Brahma, the god of creation, and said, "You made this guy. What shall I do with him?"

Brahma looked at the statute books and couldn't find a precedent to cover the case, so he said, "Take him to Krishna."

Krishna said, "The buck stops here." He examined the record very carefully and there, almost illegible, was an ancient credit entry: "Gave two cents to a beggar at the age of six."

"There," Sri Krishna said, "return his two cents and send him back to earth to try again."

Until we have learned to give freely of ourselves, we have not learned how to live.

What is here is also there; what is there,
Also here. Who sees multiplicity
But not the one indivisible Self
Must wander on and on
from death to death.

KATHA UPANISHAD

When we think of ourselves as purely physical creatures, we believe we stop with the outermost layer of our skin. Inside that boundary is home territory: there I have to consider my comforts and conveniences, my pleasure and profit foremost, because this is home. But beyond that, "It's not my problem," we say. "It's Bob's. That's *his* home, not mine."

When we live more and more for physical satisfaction, driven by this sense of otherness, we cannot help feel alienation from others. We feel estranged from others simply because we are estranged from ourselves. If we can break through to a deeper level of consciousness through the practice of meditation, we will no longer think of ourselves as merely physical. Then we will find the gap of separateness between ourselves and others becoming narrower and narrower. We get a sense of nearness to people. Where formerly we saw a chasm, now we see only a little creek; with courage, we can jump right over it.

Love, and do what you like.

SAINT AUGUSTINE

Instead of telling friends you are leading the spiritual life, which sometimes makes people raise their eyebrows, you can say, "I am learning to love." It is the same thing.

Learning to love in the way Saint Augustine is talking about is the most difficult, the most demanding, the most delightful, and the most daring of disciplines. It does not mean loving only two or three members of your family; that can often amount to building a kind of ego-annex. It does not mean loving only those who share your views, read the same newspapers, or play the same sports. Love, as Jesus puts it, means blessing those that curse you, doing good to those that hate you.

Most of us do not begin by blessing those that curse us. That is graduate school. We start with first grade – being kind to people in our family when they get resentful. Eventually comes high school, where we learn to move closer to those who are trying to shut themselves off from us. College means returning goodwill for ill will. Finally we enter graduate school: "Return love for hatred." There we learn to give our love to all – to people of different races, countries, and religions, different outlooks and strata of society, without any sense of distinction or difference.

*The tree which moves some to tears of joy
is in the eyes of others only a green thing
that stands in the way.*

WILLIAM BLAKE

One day, when I was a growing boy, my grandmother asked me a question, "Have you ever looked in Hasti's eyes?" Hasti was one of the elephants that frequently served in our religious ceremonies and that I had been learning to ride. Hasti's eyes, like the eyes of all elephants, were tiny – ridiculously small, really, for an animal so huge. "She has no idea how big she is," Granny said, "because she looks out at the world through such tiny eyes."

If the world seems hostile and lifeless, and if we seem insignificant in it, it is because, like the elephant, we look at it through such tiny eyes. Through those small eyes, shrunken by the desire for profit and personal gratification, we appear just as insignificant as all the green things – and all the other human beings, animals, fish, birds, and insects – that stand in the way.

When we are absorbed in the pursuit of profit, we live in the narrow world of the bottom line. In that world, our only neighbors are buyers and sellers, our only concerns property, profit, and possessions. Yet all around us is a world teeming with people, animals, organisms, and elements – a deeply interconnected environment that responds to all we do.

That prayer has great power which a
person makes with all his might. It makes a
sour heart sweet, a sad heart merry, a poor
heart rich, a foolish heart wise, a timid heart
brave, a sick heart well, a blind heart full
of sight, a cold heart ardent. It draws down
the great God into the little heart, it drives
the hungry soul up into the fullness
of God, it brings together two lovers,
God and the soul in a wondrous place
where they speak much of love.

MECHTHILD OF MAGDEBURG

There is nothing on earth like meditation. Each day it is new to me and fresh. I find it difficult to understand why everyone does not take to it. Millions dedicate their lives to art, music, literature, or science, which reveal just one facet of the priceless jewel hidden in the world. A life based on meditation on the Lord of Love within penetrates far beyond the multiplicity of existence into the indivisible realm of reality, where dwell infinite truth, joy, and beauty.

In meditation I see a clear, changeless goal far above the fever and fret of the day. This inner vision fills me with unshakable security, inspires me with wisdom beyond the reach of the intellect, and releases within me the capacity to act calmly and compassionately.

Seek ye first the kingdom of heaven,
and all else shall be added unto you.

THE GOSPEL ACCORDING TO
SAINT MATTHEW

The mantram is one of the best of prayers – one that we say not just when we get up or when we go to bed, but countless times throughout the day, and throughout the night as well. This prayer is not addressed to some extraterrestrial being swinging between Neptune and Pluto, but to our deepest Self, the Lord of Love, who dwells in the hearts of us all.

When we repeat the mantram, we are not asking for anything in particular, like good health or solutions to our problems or richer personal relationships. We are simply asking to get closer to the Lord, who is the source of all strength and all joy and all love. To use Jesus' words, we are asking for "the kingdom of heaven," and we find at the same time that our health improves, our problems begin to be resolved, and our relationships blossom.

*Life consists in what
a man is thinking of all day.*

RALPH WALDO EMERSON

A compulsive desire is like any other thought over which you have no control. It flows continuously: "I want that; I want that; I want that." There seems to be no space between the thoughts. But when your meditation begins to deepen, two things happen. First, the thought process slows down. Second, you develop a new attitude toward desires – you begin to realize that you needn't give in to the desire, unless you choose to. You get a taste of the powerful satisfaction that comes when you go against long-standing compulsions.

Now, when a very strong desire starts to overtake you, and your mind is just one long string of "I want that," you catch sight of a tiny opening between the demands. It may be only a split second in duration at first, but in time it grows long enough for another thought, another *kind* of thought, to make itself known. Like: "Hmmm, maybe part of me does want that – but do *I*? Is it really in my long-term best interest to gratify this desire? Or my family's?"

Blessed are the merciful:
for they shall obtain mercy.
THE GOSPEL ACCORDING TO
SAINT MATTHEW

Even if we agree with this intellectually, how many of us act as if these words apply to us? We let mercy wait while we pursue goals we understand. A luxurious home overlooking the sea through a forest of pines, prestige in our job, success for our children: don't all of us dream that such things can make us happy? We slave for them.

"That is not enough," Jesus would say quietly. Our need is for love, and we can get it only in the measure that we give. Instead of pursuing external satisfactions, we need to let love and mercy rule our decisions from day to day, and our long-range goals as well.

Then the forces of life will rise up from within to protect us. They will protect our health by keeping us clear of physical addictions and emotional obsessions. They will protect our mind by keeping it calm and detached. People will surround us with affection and support when they see we care about them more than we do about ourselves.

*We need men who can dream of things
that never were, and ask why not.*

GEORGE BERNARD SHAW

In an Indian movie I saw recently, a villager leaves home for the first time to travel to the city of Bombay. When he returns, his family and friends crowd around him, asking what it was like in the big city. His laconic reply sums up our era: "Such tall buildings . . . and such small people."

If we were asked to give an accounting of our society's achievements, we could claim many great technological developments and scientific discoveries, plenty of skyscrapers, and the amassment of huge sums of money, but few truly secure, truly wise, truly great men and women. It is not for lack of ability or energy, though; it is because we lack a noble goal.

To grow to our full height, we need to be challenged with tasks that draw out our deeper resources, the talents and capacities we did not know we had. We need to be faced with obstacles that cannot be surmounted unless we summon up every last ounce of our daring and creativity. This kind of challenge is familiar to any great athlete or scientist or artist. No truly worthwhile accomplishment comes easily.

To be sure, this requires effort and love, a
careful cultivation of the spiritual life, and a
watchful, honest, active oversight of all one's
mental attitudes towards things and people.
It is not to be learned by world-flight,
running away from things, turning solitary
and going apart from the world. Rather,
one must learn an inner solitude, wherever
or with whomsoever he may be. He
must learn to penetrate things and find
God there, to get a strong impression
of God firmly fixed on his mind.

MEISTER ECKHART

To give full attention to whatever you are doing isn't at all easy. When we have a job we dislike, or must work with people who are difficult, most of us become like children – looking at this glass for a moment, then at this table, then out the window; then when there is nothing else to look at, we start crying. If we could only attend a little more to the work, even when we dislike it, it would become quite interesting.

When we can give it our full attention, anything becomes interesting. And anything, when we do not give it our full attention, becomes uninteresting.

*O Krishna, the stillness of divine
union which you describe is beyond my
comprehension. How can the mind, which
is so restless, attain lasting peace? Krishna,
the mind is restless, turbulent, powerful,
violent; trying to control it is like trying
to tame the wind.*

ARJUNA (BHAGAVAD GITA)

I like to think of the mind as the Big Boss, and
the senses as his five secretaries. In any bureau-
cracy it's difficult to go directly to the boss. If
he's a busy man -- and the mind is surely that!
... with lots of appointments, lots of high-level
negotiations on his hands – you are wise to start
by winning the goodwill of his secretaries.

For a long time the situation resembles those
movies from the 1930's where Spencer Tracy
breezes into the office, flings himself onto a corner of the receptionist's desk, and turns on the
charm: "Hey, Honey, how's the Bossman
today?" She gives him an icy look. But gradually
the ice melts and the secretary becomes the
staunch ally.

To win over the senses, when they're clamoring for the second piece of pie, or a cigarette and
a stiff drink, you'll need more than Hollywood
charm. You will need the systematic practice of
meditation and the other spiritual disciplines. If
you want to be admitted to the Boss's office,
you'll have to persevere over a long period of
time. And if you want to be the Boss's Boss, that
will require a lot of hard, hard work on the spiritual path.

What a man takes in by contemplation,
that he pours out in love.

MEISTER ECKHART

The old dispute about the relative virtues of the active way to spiritual awareness versus the contemplative way is a spurious one. We require both. They are phases of a single rhythm like the pulsing of the heart, the in-drawing and letting go of breath, the ebb and flow of the tides. So we go deep, turned inwards in meditation to consolidate our vital energy, and then with greater love and wisdom we come out into the family, the community, the world. Without action we lack opportunities for changing our old ways, and we increase our self-will rather than lessen it; without contemplation we lack the strength to change and are blown about by our conditioning. When we meditate every day and also do our best in every situation, we walk both worthy roads, the *via contemplativa* and the *via activa*.

The world is too much with us;
late and soon,
Getting and spending,
we lay waste our powers:
Little we see in Nature that is ours.

WILLIAM WORDSWORTH

Our modern way of life seems to be making us busier and busier about less and less. It is only after we begin to taste the joy of simple living that we realize all this frantic activity can stand between us and our fulfillment. The more we divide our interests, our allegiances, our activities, the less time we have for living.

Loving, loyal personal relationships take time. We cannot get to know someone intimately in a day or establish a lasting relationship during a weekend conference. If we spend eight hours a day at our job, and the evening watching television, where is the time for cultivating close friendships?

If we simplify our lives, we shall find the time and energy to be together with our family and friends, or to give our time to a worthy cause that needs our contribution. The simple life doesn't mean bearing with a drab routine; it means giving our time and attention to what is most important.

*My life is an indivisible whole, and all
my attitudes run into one another;
and they all have their rise in my
insatiable love for mankind.*

MAHATMA GANDHI

We should be able to make all sorts of graceful concessions on things that do not matter in life – and yet stand unshakable on essentials. To do this, we have to be detached from our opinions. I'm not recommending that we be wishy-washy, or lacking in strong opinions on basic issues, but that we cultivate the forbearance not to force our opinions on others.

When we have strength of conviction we will not get rattled when people question or contradict us. Mahatma Gandhi, for example, was not in favor of tea or coffee, but he took joy in making a cup of tea for his wife each morning just the way she liked it. This is bending gracefully on nonessentials. When it came to essentials, however, Gandhi was unshakable. His dedication to nonviolence was so absolute that he would abruptly call off a successful nationwide program of noncooperation with the British if he heard any reports of violence committed by his countrymen, even those who did not acknowledge him as their leader.

*This gift is from God and not of man's
deserving. But certainly no one ever receives
such a great grace without tremendous
labor and burning desire.*

RICHARD OF SAINT-VICTOR

The grace of the Lord is like a wind that is blowing all the time, but it is our responsibility to get rid of our excess luggage and set our sail correctly. For a long time in meditation we are merely bailing out the boat and throwing things overboard. We begin by throwing out things we have become tired of, things to which we are not very attached. If I have two sets of the *Encyclopaedia Britannica*, I can give you one.

The second stage is harder; then we must begin to throw away some of the things to which we are attached. A tussle ensues, an inner conflict: to throw or not to throw is the question.

But in the final stages, when we see the lights on the other shore, when we see Jesus walking about, the Buddha meditating, and Sri Krishna playing on the flute, all we want is to get to where the action is. At that time, even selfish people like you and me, who have committed many mistakes in their ignorance, want to get there so fast that they take hold of everything – their glasses, the shirt on their back, even the sail and rudder – and start throwing it all overboard. In the final stages, the great difficulty is to persuade people to keep a few things. After all, if you don't have your glasses, how will you see the Lord?

He that can have patience,
can have what he will.

BENJAMIN FRANKLIN

Here is a tip for keeping the palate on the middle path. When it is craving candy or a hot fudge sundae, go for a walk repeating the mantram, and bargain for time. Tell your mind, "In two hours, on our way home we can go to an ice cream parlor for a deluxe sundae." Interestingly enough, two hours later the mind has forgotten ice cream sundaes and is thinking about the movie it will enjoy tomorrow evening. All you need do is put just a little break of time between the palate and its desire, for you can count on the mind to change its desires.

Treat the mind gently, patiently, and compassionately. Since we have allowed it license for so many years, it is not fair to expect it to come round in a day or two.

A human being has so many skins inside,
covering the depths of the heart. We know
so many things, but we don't know
ourselves! Why, thirty or forty skins or
hides, as thick and hard as an ox's or a bear's,
cover the soul. Go into your own ground and
learn to know yourself there.

MEISTER ECKHART

Below the relatively superficial levels of the mind – beneath the emotions we are ordinarily aware of – lie layer on layer of the unconscious mind. This is the "cloud of unknowing," where primordial instincts, fears, and urges cover our understanding so that we see nothing except ourselves. The deepest flaw in the mind is what Einstein called the "kind of optical delusion of consciousness" that makes us see ourselves as separate from the rest of life. Like a crack in glasses that we must wear every moment of our lives, this division is built into the mind. "I" versus "not-I" runs through everything we see.

To see life as it is, the mind must be made pure – everything that distorts must be quieted or removed. When the mind is completely still, unstirred even in its depths, we see straight through to the ground of our being, which is divine.

*Strength does not come from physical
capacity. It comes from an indomitable will.*

MAHATMA GANDHI

What counts most in life is not IQ, but WQ,
"Will Quotient." No one can plead that he or
she lacks will. There is will in every desire. Every
desire carries with it the will to bring that desire
to fruition. When it comes to something we like,
we have all the will we need. Someone says,
"Hey, come on, we're going skiing!" and that is
enough. We will get out of bed at three in the
morning, drive for hours, stand cheerfully in the
snow waiting for the ski lift, and in general suffer
all kinds of discomfort with a will of iron. Yet as
small a challenge as a letter to Aunt Gertrude will
find the will against us.

To control our destiny, we need to harness
our will, to do not what we *like*, but what is in
our long-term best interest. If the will is strong
enough, anything can be accomplished; if the
will is weak, very little. In every endeavor, it is
the man or woman with an unbreakable will
who excels.

As an eagle, weary after soaring in the sky,
folds its wings and flies down to rest in its
nest, so does the shining Self enter the
state of dreamless sleep, where one is
freed from all desires.

BRIHADARANYAKA UPANISHAD

In meditation it is very important right from the outset to get into the habit of keeping the spinal column erect. Head, neck, and spine should be naturally in a straight line. This does not mean making your body tense. Straining physically makes you acutely aware of the body, which defeats the purpose of meditation. But on the other hand, do not let the body slump; that is inviting sleep to come and carry you away. If you feel yourself growing drowsy, draw yourself up straight and let the wave of sleep pass over you.

After a lot of sustained, systematic effort in meditation, we may finally succeed in breaking through the surface crust of consciousness. What lies below is the unconscious, which has many layers – strata on strata deposited by habits of thinking and acting, little by little, every day of our life. Every time we try to pierce through to a deeper level, the mind is likely to fall asleep.

A very pleasant wave of sleep seems to engulf you, but if you want to go deeper in meditation, you must learn to remain alert at this time. Drilling through these strata in meditation means overcoming limitations, all the obstacles created by self-will.

Those whose consciousness is unified
abandon all attachment to the results
of action and attain supreme peace. But
those whose desires are fragmented,
who are selfishly attached to the results of
their work, are bound in everything they do.

SRI KRISHNA (BHAGAVAD GITA)

To have courage for whatever comes in life –
everything lies in that.

SAINT TERESA OF AVILA

It is not so much work that tires us, as ego-driven work. When we are selfishly involved, we cannot help worrying, we cannot help getting overly concerned about our success or failure. It is the preoccupation with results that makes us tense. Our very anxiety exhausts us.

For the majority of us, uncertainty is worse than disaster: disaster comes to us only rarely; worry depletes us often. We never know whether we are going to get a brick or a bouquet. If we knew for certain a brick was on its way, there would be no anxiety. We would just say, "Throw it and be done with it."

We should learn how to handle both bricks and bouquets, praise and censure, success and defeat. When we can say, "Whatever disasters come, we will not be afraid because the Lord is within us," then this resoluteness and faith will enable us to work free from tension, agitation, and fear of defeat. The person who works with this attitude is always at peace, because he is not anxious about the results of his action.

*The little unremembered acts of kindness
and love are the best of a good man's life.*
WILLIAM WORDSWORTH

Our lives affect others, whether directly, through the environment, or by the force of our example. For instance, we could say that smoking shows a lack of love: first, because our capacity for love is actually caught in the compulsion to smoke; but more than that, the example tells even casual passers-by, "Don't worry about the surgeon general. Don't worry about the consequences. If it feels good, do it!"

Pele, the Brazilian soccer star, has long been in a position to command a king's ransom for endorsing commercial products. He has never given his endorsement to any cigarette, putting the reason in simple words: "I love kids." That is a perfect choice of words. He *does* love kids. He knows that in most of the world they will buy anything with his name on it. Therefore, though he came from a poor family, no amount of money can tempt him to do something that will mislead young people or injure their health.

To love is to be responsible like this in everything: the work we do, the things we buy, the food we eat, the people we look up to, the movies we see, the words we use, every choice we make from morning till night. That is the real measure of love; it is a wonderfully demanding responsibility.

*The intellect is weak; it has no power
except over what is as weak as itself.*

AL-NURI

*The sage awakes to light in the night of
all creatures. That which the world calls day
is the night of ignorance to the wise.*

SRI KRISHNA (BHAGAVAD GITA)

When I go into a movie theater for a bargain matinee, for a few moments I can't see a thing. My eyes, used to the dazzling California sunlight, are temporarily rendered useless, and I have no idea where to find a seat. This is somewhat the way it feels to plunge below the level of discursive thought in meditation: you don't see anything that looks like life as we know it, and you feel blind and confused. You are entering the unconscious, trying to become conscious, and everything is unfamiliar.

Spiritual teachers function somewhat like movie ushers who come up to us in the darkness and say, "Do you see that corner there? Fourth row to the left; there's a seat right by the aisle." We stand still for a few minutes, and soon we can make out a few heads directly in front. Finally we can see the seats and reach them without stumbling. The same thing happens in meditation; it is simply a matter of training our inward eye.

*Man goes far away or near but God never
goes far off; he is always standing close at
hand, and even if he cannot stay within
he goes no further than the door.*

MEISTER ECKHART

It is so easy to repeat the mantram that at first most of us cannot believe that it is charged with great power. Only after we use it for a while do we begin to see that repeating the mantram is not just a mechanical exercise; it is a direct line to the Lord within, somewhat like picking up the phone and calling the Lord collect. We don't have to make any promises or commitments; we only have to repeat the Holy Name when we are agitated – angry, afraid, speeded up, or caught in worries or regrets – and the Lord opens a little door to the reserves of our deeper consciousness.

Have patience with all things, but
chiefly have patience with yourself. Do not
lose courage in considering your own
imperfections, but instantly set about
remedying them – every day
begin the task anew.

SAINT FRANCIS DE SALES

While we were living on the Blue Mountain in India, we noticed that our local bank had a very neighborly arrangement for collecting funds from the villagers. Poor villagers have very little to save, only a few copper pennies at most. To encourage them to deposit even these few pennies every day, the bank employed a boy with a bicycle to go into the village to their homes, collect their few coppers, and enter the total in their account.

In meditation it is the same: when the Lord comes, we can say, "We are no great mystic, but a few times today we have tried to be patient. A few times today we have tried to put our family first. A few times today we have resisted some little craving for personal satisfaction."

This is how most of us are going to lead the spiritual life for a long time: a few pennies here, a few pennies there, collected every day. But in these innumerable little acts of selflessness lies spiritual growth, which over a long period can transform every one of us into a loving person. To quote the bank advertisement, "It all adds up."

Whatever you do, make it an offering to me
– the food you eat, the sacrifices you make,
the help you give, even your suffering.

SRI KRISHNA (BHAGAVAD GITA)

We can't give anyone joy or security by increasing her bank account or adding to his collection of vintage wines. Of course, a well-chosen gift given at the right time is not out of place, but whatever the gift, we should guard against the nagging expectation of getting something in return. The moment you expect reward or recognition, you are making a contract.

Even parents and children suffer from this contractual relationship. Parents can help their children tremendously by avoiding the "I did this for you, therefore you do that for me" approach, encouraging them instead to follow their own star. In the spiritual lore of India, it is said that the Lord whispered only one word in our ears when he sent us into the world: "Give." Give freely of your time, your talent, your resources; give without asking for anything in return. This is the secret of living in joy and security.

Sin is whatever obscures the soul.

ANDRE GIDE

In India there is a saying that Rama, the principle of abiding joy, and Kama, selfish desire, cannot live together. This is difficult for most of us to understand because we usually feel that even if Rama has to be brought in, Kama can be given a little closet, or some little corner behind a curtain so that he isn't visible. Every mystic worth the name says it must be Rama *or* Kama; we cannot have both together.

But let's remember that we have to be prepared for a long period of development before Kama finally packs up his belongings and leaves without any forwarding address. Let's not get agitated if, after a long time on the spiritual path, we still feel some of our old cravings. As our spiritual awareness deepens, we will come not to identify ourselves with those desires. Then a big desire may pop out and crawl like a rat across the stage of our consciousness, but we will just calmly sit and watch. Until this blessed day of detachment dawns, I would suggest that when old desires and urges visit us, the very best way to deal with them is go for a long, brisk walk repeating the mantram.

Sages speak of the immutable
Tree of Life, with its taproot above
and its branches below.

SRI KRISHNA (BHAGAVAD GITA)

Most of this Tree of Life is not physical. The whole phenomenal universe – matter, energy, and mind – is only its canopy of countless little leaves. This is all we can see. But each leaf grows from a twig, which grows from a branch, which in turn grows from a vast trunk. And supporting the trunk and all its leaves and twigs and branches – completely hidden – is the taproot, extending deep into pure being. The taproot of this tree is the Lord, the eternal, changeless Self.

This image is more than poetry: it is personal and practical. As long as we live on the surface of life, we believe we are separate, individual leaves. We lead private lives that bear little relation to the rest of the tree, even though when we are cut off from that tree we have no life. Driven by self-will, we cannot imagine we are forfeiting the whole of life for the little leaf we call our individual personality. So when you get up in the morning, remind yourself of this magnificent simile, which asks us to claim the whole Tree of Life and not be content with being one seasonal leaf.

A mind that is fast is sick.
A mind that is slow is sound.
A mind that is still is divine.

MEHER BABA

Somehow, in our modern civilization, we have acquired the idea that the mind is working best when it runs at top speed. Yet a racing mind lacks time even to finish a thought, let alone to check on its quality. When we slow down the mind, we work better at everything we do. Not only is the quality of our work better, we are actually able to get more done. A calm, smooth-running flow of thought saves a lot of wear and tear on the nervous system, which means you have more vitality and resilience in the face of stress.

Say to my brethren when they see me dead
and weep for me, lamenting me in sadness:
"Think ye I am this corpse ye are to bury?
I swear by God, this dead one is not I.
When I had formal shape, then this,
my body, served as my garment,
I wore it for a while."

AL-GHAZALI

In the midst of life we are in death.

BOOK OF COMMON PRAYER

Death is not an event which takes place on a particular day in a particular place. Every moment that passes brings us that much closer to the day this body will be taken away from us. The cells of the body are dying every second, but the limits of our vision keep us from seeing that the body we identify with is in a constant state of change. Those who are sensitive to this have tremendous motivation to take to the spiritual path.

The Buddhas do but tell the way,
it is for you to swelter at the task.

THE BUDDHA

Spiritual teachers are like signposts pointing the way to immortality, but it is we who must make the journey. This is quite reasonable. After all, when we pass a signpost on the freeway, we don't expect it to get into the driver's seat and do the driving while we lie down in the back to take a nap. On the first half of the spiritual journey, we cannot expect other people to pick us up and carry us along. It is up to us to meditate regularly, and practice the allied disciplines.

Sri Ramakrishna says that the first part of the trip is the "way of the monkey." The little baby monkey has to hold on for dear life while his mother swings from tree to tree. If the little one loses his grip, he'll fall and hurt himself. But the second half is the "way of the cat." The little kitten just sits there on the road looking cute and helpless, saying, "mew, mew, mew," and the mother cat picks it up by the scruff of its neck and takes it to safety. It is only on the second half of the journey that we are carried by a power higher than ourselves. Still, I would add that even though the Lord may be carrying us, he is not going to coddle us. If we even think of straying away, he will hit us hard, to remind us of his presence. That is how he shows his love.

He who holds back rising anger like a
rolling chariot, him I call a real driver;
other people are but holding the reins.

THE BUDDHA

It takes two to quarrel: the other person can throw down the gauntlet, but we don't have to pick it up. When someone criticizes us or contradicts us or speaks in an unpleasant tone of voice, there is no quarrel as long as we remember that we have the choice not to reply in the same manner.

Trouble starts only when we react on the stimulus and response level of tit for tat – which may be all right for two-year-olds but not for mature men and women. If we can remember the mantram at such times, it will help us to be more patient, and our example will help the other person to be more patient too.

*When we thus clear the ground and make
our soul ready, without doubt God must fill
up the void. . . . If you go out of yourself,
without doubt he shall go in, and there will
be much or little of his entering in according
to how much or little you go out.*

JOHANNES TAULER

*God expects but one thing of you, and
that is that you should come out of
yourself in so far as you are a created
being and let God be God in you.*

MEISTER ECKHART

In those moments when we forget ourselves –
not thinking, "Am I happy?" but completely
oblivious to our little ego – we spend a brief but
beautiful holiday in heaven. The mystics tell us
that the joy we experience in these moments of
self-forgetting is our true nature, our native
state. To regain it, we have simply to empty ourselves of what hides this joy: that is, to stop
dwelling on ourselves. To the extent that we are
not full of ourselves, God can fill us – in fact, the
mystics say daringly, he *has* to.

The first wealth is health.

RALPH WALDO EMERSON

When you regard your life as a trust, you realize that the first resource you have to take care of is your own body. This can be startling. Even your body is not really your own. It belongs to life, and it is your responsibility to take care of it. You cannot afford to do anything that injures your body, because the body is the instrument you need for selfless action. That is the fine print of the trust agreement: when we smoke, when we overeat, when we don't get enough exercise, we are violating the terms of the trust.

If you want to live life at its fullest, you will want to do everything possible to keep your body in vibrant health in order to give back to life a little of what it has given you.

*If a man who enjoys a lesser happiness
beholds a greater one, let him leave aside
the lesser to gain the greater.*

THE BUDDHA

The Buddha, the most practical of teachers, says that wisdom is essentially discrimination – the precious capacity to see what is important in the long run and to choose our course of action accordingly.

Most of us are vigilant when making big decisions, but less so when dealing with little ones. We forget the cumulative effect of all those missed "little" opportunities. It is precisely on those thousand little occasions, and over a period of time, that the mind is taught to be calm and kind – not instantaneously or by great leaps. In the ordinary choices of every day we begin to change the direction of our lives.

*I desire not to desire, for my will is
without value, since I am ignorant in any
case. Therefore choose Thou for me what
Thou knowest to be best and do not put
my perdition in what my autonomy
and free choice prefer.*

BAYAZID AL-BISTAMI

Sometimes we make a little wall around ourselves by saying, "I want this particular pleasure *here*, where I can enjoy it all for myself. I don't want to share it with anybody outside." While we are walling pleasure in, we are walling others out.

That is why the pursuit of personal pleasure makes us more alienated and estranged. After some years, the wall of selfishness can become a prison. All of us know people who can think of no one else's feelings but their own; their later years are full of loneliness and estrangement. When we refrain from acting on a negative emotion or selfish desire, we stop building the wall around our life – we can open our life up to others.

He who interrupts the course of his
spiritual exercises and prayer is like a man
who allows a bird to escape from his
hand; he can hardly catch it again.

SAINT JOHN OF THE CROSS

Try to have your meditation at the same time every day. It is very much like dinner. When you have been eating at 6:30 every evening for a year or so, your stomach no longer has to ask if it is time to punch in. When 6:30 approaches, it knows the time has come for action. Similarly, if you have been having morning and evening meditation regularly, even if the mind has been unruly the rest of the day, it knows these are times to quiet down. After a while this becomes a precious habit. Just as at 6:10 you begin to feel hungry for lasagna, in the morning you will feel a kind of mental hunger for meditation.

True love grows by sacrifice and
the more thoroughly the soul rejects
natural satisfaction the stronger and
more detached its tenderness becomes.

SAINT THERESE OF LISIEUX

If somebody is kind to us ninety-nine times and then does one hurtful thing, we are likely to forget the ninety-nine good things and remember the one bad thing. We can watch it happen in ourselves – no matter how absurd we know it is – when our parents or partner or children fail us and we blow a fuse. When we get angry, we suffer a curious, temporary attack of amnesia. For the time being, we just cannot remember those two weeks she nursed us when we came down with viral flu. We forget the time he entertained us cheerfully when we were depressed and irritable. We don't see the hundreds and hundreds of white flags charting the course of good relations down the years. We see only this last crimson flag waving menacingly in our face.

This is not to say that we should close our eyes when someone is unkind to us. But if, with the help of the mantram, we can turn our attention away from that one act of unkindness and turn it to all the kindnesses we have received down the years, the incident will fall into its proper place. We will probably say to ourselves, "This hostility is so petty! I shouldn't even have let it come up."

Nonviolence is the supreme law of life.
HINDU PROVERB

The Sanskrit word for nonviolence is *ahimsa:* *a-* means "not" or "without"; *himsa* is violence. This may sound negative, but in Sanskrit a word constructed in this way stands for a state both perfect and positive. Ahimsa implies that when every trace of violence is removed from the mind, what is left is our natural state of consciousness: pure love. Unfortunately, that love has been buried under layer upon layer of ill will and selfish conditioning. To have love bubble up to the surface of our life, all we have to do is systematically remove all those layers.

There are three kinds of violence: one, through our deeds; two, through our words; and three, through our thoughts. Most of what we call violence is in the form of action, and it is with our actions that nonviolence naturally begins. But as long as our minds harbor violent thoughts, that incipient violence will find its way somehow into our speech and behavior. The root of all violence is in the world of thoughts, and that is why training the mind is so important.

There is hunger for ordinary bread,
and there is hunger for love, for kindness, for
thoughtfulness; and this is the great poverty
that makes people suffer so much.

MOTHER TERESA OF CALCUTTA

Our modern civilization is so physically oriented that when we hear the word *hunger*, we immediately think of vitamins and minerals and amino acids. It seldom occurs to us that just as the body develops problems when it does not get adequate food, the person who is deprived of love – or worse, who finds it difficult to love – becomes subject to problems every bit as serious.

This doesn't mean just emotional problems, which of course are included. More and more evidence indicates that lack of love not only leads to loneliness, despair, and resentment, but also contributes to the deterioration of physical health. When spiritual figures like Mother Teresa talk about our need to love and to be loved, the need is not metaphorical. She is not talking about some vague spirituality; she is talking about good nutrition. Resentment, hostility, alienation, and selfishness are deficiency diseases. You can have all the essential amino acids, vitamins, and minerals known and unknown but if you cannot love, you are not likely to remain in good health.

*Just as there is no loss of basic energy in
the universe, so no thought or action is
without its effects, present or ultimate,
seen or unseen, felt or unfelt.*

NORMAN COUSINS

Just as the example of Jesus inspired Francis of Assisi a millennium later, Francis inspired thousands of people during his own lifetime, and continues to do so today. Francis was recognized as a powerful preacher, but it was his simple and selfless life that moved hearts. It was his life, and his experience of God, that gave power to his words.

Near the end of his life, while he was making a mountain journey, Francis's health failed. His companions went into a farmyard to borrow a donkey for him to ride. On hearing for whom it was intended, the peasant came out and asked, "Are you the Brother Francis there is so much said about?" Receiving a nod from one of Francis's companions, he added, "Then take care that you are as good in reality as they say, for there are many who have confidence in you." Deeply stirred, Francis kissed the peasant in gratitude for this reminder.

We are not poor friars living in medieval Italy, but the lesson is the same: let us remember that our lives set an example for others. No one can say his life doesn't matter, her words don't matter.

*The time of business does not with me
differ from the time of prayer, and in the
noise and clatter of my kitchen, while
several persons are at the same time calling
for different things, I possess God in as
great tranquility as if I were upon my
knees at the blessed sacrament.*

BROTHER LAWRENCE

The mind has a tremendous natural capacity to dwell on things, and in repeating the mantram we are channeling this capacity to train the mind. It is the same capacity, only we are giving it a different focus. There is a story in the Hasidic tradition of Judaism in which a man asks his *zaddik* or spiritual teacher, "Do you mean we should remember the Lord even in the give-and-take of business?" "Yes, of course," the rabbi replies. "If we can remember business matters in the hour of prayer, shouldn't we be able to remember God in the transactions of our business?"

When thou art quiet and silent, then art
thou as God was before nature and creature;
thou art that which God then was; thou
art that whereof he made thy nature and
creature: Then thou hearest and seest even
with that wherewith God himself saw and
heard in thee, before ever thine own
willing or thine own seeing began.

JACOB BOEHME

In our half hour of meditation, we may have
only a minute or two of real concentration, but
that minute or two is tremendous. The rushing,
turbulent process we call the mind has almost
come to a healing halt. In those few minutes all
kinds of changes take place throughout the
body and the mind. The breathing rhythm may
fall drastically. Other biological processes are
slowed down, without our being aware of it. It
is such a deeply restful, renewing state that after
a taste of it, we will want it again so badly that we
will do everything we can during the rest of the
day to make our next period of meditation
deeper. One minute of this experience is worth
hours of disciplining the mind. But we do not get
that minute until we have trained the mind to
quiet down.

*Be vigilant; guard your mind
against negative thoughts.*
THE BUDDHA

Today, many people are very well-informed about nutrition. We worry about "junk food," which is a legitimate concern, but shouldn't we be just as worried by the low-grade food we sometimes feed our minds? There is junk food, yes. But there are also "junk thoughts."

Take a close look at the entertainment pages of your newspaper, for example. We have become so used to this kind of fare that we seldom even question it. I can imagine what people who lived in the Dark Ages would say if they saw today's paper from the Bay Area: "They think *we* lived in the Dark Ages! What about them?" Millions of people spend hours every day feeding their minds and the minds of their children with unadulterated junk.

It is not just a few nude scenes or explicit language, which are often more juvenile than alarming, but the terribly unkind attitudes people display toward each other on the screen, on stage, and on the printed page, which they vent in harsh words and harmful acts. All this goes into our minds and gets absorbed; it cannot help but resurface in our behavior. It is not that we want to live in a germ-free world, which is impossible, but we need to remember that mental states are affected by what we see, hear, and read every day.

*If the heart wanders or is distracted, bring it
back to the point quite gently and replace it
tenderly in its Master's presence. And even if
you did nothing during the whole of your
hour but bring your heart back and place it
again in Our Lord's presence, though it went
away every time you brought it back, your
hour would be very well employed.*

SAINT FRANCIS DE SALES

The mind does not like to meditate; it wants to
wander. When someone is not doing very well in
meditation, one explanation is simple: his or her
mind is elsewhere. The early stages of meditation are like a primary school for the mind. At
first we are simply trying to get the mind to stay
on the school grounds until the last bell rings.
This is all we can do at first. The mind has been
playing truant for years; when we try to concentrate, it simply is not present. All we can do is
stand at the doorstep and whistle, trying to call it
back in.

Even if all we do in thirty minutes of meditation is to call the mind back thirty times, we have
made great progress. We don't have to wait for
the day when the mind is completely still to receive immense benefits from meditation. As the
Bhagavad Gita says, even a little of this discipline protects us from great dangers.

Households, cities, countries, and nations have enjoyed great happiness when a single individual has taken heed of the Good and Beautiful. . . .Such men not only liberate themselves; they fill those they meet with a free mind.

PHILO

Just as we live in a physical atmosphere, we are surrounded also by a mental atmosphere. And just as the air we breathe may become polluted, our mental atmosphere can be polluted by negative thinking.

If trees were not always releasing oxygen into the atmosphere, scientists tell us, all life on earth would suffer. On a smoggy day in California, the trees along the freeway look gray and drab in the haze; they do not seem to add anything valuable to the landscape. Yet they are performing a vital function: they are taking in our carbon dioxide and giving us oxygen in return.

A person whose mind is free from negative thinking spreads a life-giving influence in much the same way that a tree gives oxygen. Although a selfless man or woman may seem to go through the day doing nothing extraordinary, without them nothing would revitalize the atmosphere in which we think. By being vigilant, and not encouraging negative thoughts, all of us can offer this vital service – which benefits everybody, including ourselves.

The disunited mind is far from wise;
how can it meditate? How be at peace?
When you know no peace,
how can you know joy?

SRI KRISHNA (BHAGAVAD GITA)

Today's mania for speed strikes right at the root of our capacity for an even mind. How often we find ourselves locked into behavior and situations that force us to hurry, hurry, hurry! By now, most of us are aware that compulsive speed – "hurry sickness" – can be a direct threat to our physical health. But hurry has another alarming repercussion: it cripples patience.

When we lack patience even a few moments' delay, a trivial disappointment, an unexpected obstacle, makes us explode in anger. We are not hostile people; we are just in such a hurry that keeping the mind calm is impossible. Without peace of mind, how can we enjoy anything, from a movie to good health?

When we go slower, we are more patient, and when we are more patient, we are capable of enjoying life more. All these benefits can come from just learning to slow down.

*Thou shalt understand that it is a science
most profitable, and passing all other
sciences, for to learn to die. For a man to
know that he shall die, that is common to all
men; as much as there is no man that may
ever live or he hath hope or trust thereof; but
thou shalt find full few that hath this cunning
to learn to die. . . . I shall give thee the
mystery of this doctrine; the which shall
profit thee greatly to the beginning of
ghostly health, and to a stable
fundament of all virtues.*

HEINRICH SUSO

As long as there is something we want to get out
of life before we go – a little more money, a little
more pleasure, a chance to get in a parting dig at
someone we think has hurt us – there will be a
terrible struggle with death when it comes. As
long as we think we are the body, we will fight
tooth and nail to hold on to the body when death
comes to wrench it away. The tragedy, of
course, is that death is going to take it anyway.
So the great mystics all tell us, "Give up your
selfish attachments now and be free." Then,
when Death does come, we can give him what is
his without a shadow of regret, and keep for ourselves what is ours, which is love of the Lord.

There is great artistry in this. Death comes
and growls something about how our time has
come, and we just say, "Don't growl; I'm ready
to come on my own." Then we stand up gracefully, take off the jacket that is the body, place it
carefully in Death's arms and go home.

*Progress in meditation comes swiftly
for those who try their hardest.*

PATANJALI

Given the sheer impossibility of it, I always find it astonishing how swiftly the transformation of personality can proceed when we are meditating with sustained enthusiasm. It may have taken you thirty years to make yourself resentful, but in much less than thirty years you can become secure, loving, resilient. The key is simple: how much do we *desire* to change?

Patanjali, who was one of the foremost teachers of meditation in ancient India, makes a deceptively simple understatement: they go fastest who try hardest. Whether it is tennis or transformation, the secret is the same: to achieve success, we need to master our desires.

If thou canst walk on water
Thou art no better than a straw.
If thou canst fly in the air
Thou art no better than a fly.
Conquer thy heart
That thou mayest become somebody.

ANSARI

Sometimes we are advised to let our frustrations express themselves when they build up. One of the biggest problems with this advice is that by venting negative feelings, we relive them – confirming our suspicions that an angry man or petulant woman is who we really are. This is a most devitalizing self-image. We may not even like such a person, but if we are not vigilant, we can reach a stage where we throw up our hands and say: "This is the real me; what can I do?"

To establish a more positive identity, we need a good deal of patience and a certain sagacious realism. On the one hand, it does no good to pretend that simply because we are made in the image of the Lord, our problems are not really there. We should be prepared to see our difficulties as clearly as possible, so that we do everything we can to work on them. But on the other hand, we should not allow ourselves to be overwhelmed by them. Meditation gradually clears our eyes, deepens our security, and releases tremendous resources to solve our problems.

Nothing can throw thee into the
infernal abyss so much as this detested
word – heed well! – this mine and thine.

ANGELUS SILESIUS

The man or woman of God is not misled by cosmologies that place hell in the bowels of the earth or heaven at the farthest reaches of the galaxies. Heaven does exist, they maintain, and hell is as real as Paris or Cincinnati. Both heaven and hell are right at hand. From one moment to the next we can choose in which one we will dwell, because they are not geographical locations – they are states of consciousness. Two people may be next-door neighbors: to one, their little condominium may be paradise; to the other it may be a teeming web of emotional intrigue, suspicion, and envy – in short, hell.

For anyone who has realized the unity of life, awareness of that unity is heaven. The keenest anguish such a person can imagine would be to plunge back for even a moment into narrower vision.

*The true saint goes in and out amongst the
people and eats and sleeps with them and
buys and sells in the market and marries and
takes part in social intercourse, and never
forgets God for a single moment.*

ABU SA'ID

There are some who like to imagine themselves
as pilgrims moving among the deer on high forest paths, simply clad, sipping only pure head-
waters, breathing only ethereal mountain air. To
meditate and live the spiritual life, we needn't
drop everything and undertake an ascent of the
Himalayas or Mount Athos or Cold Mountain.
It may not sound glamorous, but you can actually do better right where you are.

Your situation may lack the grandeur of those
austere and solitary peaks, but it could be a very
fertile valley yielding marvelous fruit. We need
people if we are to grow, and all our problems
with them, properly seen, are opportunities for
growth. Can you practice patience with a deer?
Can you learn to forgive a redwood? Trying to
live in harmony with those around you right
now will bring out enormous inner toughness.

I have joined my heart to Thee: all that
exists are Thou. O Lord, beloved of my
heart, Thou art the home of all;
Where indeed is the heart in which
Thou dost not dwell?

JAFAR

Loving someone does not mean automatically acquiescing to their every whim. Sometimes love shows itself in saying "no" to an attitude or desire that is harmful. But your opposing must be done tenderly, without anger or condescension. This is a difficult art.

Go slowly. Remember that it is better not to react in the heat of the moment. Whenever time allows, don't respond immediately. Speak and act when you can do so with patience and kindness. Remember, too, that the very best way to change someone is to embody that change with your own example.

Great lovers of god, like Saint Teresa of Avila or Mahatma Gandhi, see the Lord in the heart of every person around them. This is the vision that enables them to treat others with love and respect even in the heat of opposition. It may take time, but no one is immune to this kind of love.

*Place yourself as an instrument
in the hands of God who does his
own work in his own way.*

SWAMI RAMDAS

To spend a certain amount of time working with people at some job that benefits others, in which our personal pleasure and profit are not at all involved, nourishes both us and the people we help. It helps them directly, but it helps us indirectly, by enabling us to realize that we are a part of life, not just a separate, selfish fragment.

Today, there are so many places where help is needed. Open the daily paper – the news speaks for itself. All of us need to work together to put out the fires of hatred and violence that are burning throughout the world, threatening us and our children. I cannot imagine any human being who has love in his heart not trying to think of ways to make some contribution to the world. We needn't work on a large scale. The important thing is that each of us give some time to working for a selfless cause. It's good for the world, and it's good for us.

*The philosopher is Nature's pilot. And
there you have our difference: to be in hell is
to drift: to be in heaven is to steer.*

GEORGE BERNARD SHAW

The real issue in life is choice. If you had a car
that could only turn one way, would you say
that it is free? If it ran around crashing into
things, denting its fenders and wasting all its
fuel, would you shrug and say, "That's the auto-
motive nature. That's my car's mode of self-expression?" It would take you a long time to get
anywhere, and where you arrived would not be
up to you.

The other day I set out for a drive through the
California wine country. With a car that did not
obey me, I might have ended up about a hundred
miles away at the River's End restaurant, where
the Russian River empties into the sea. It is
tragic, but many lives are like that. At the end of
the line there is nothing to do but go inside, get
something hot to drink, and recall a line or two
from Swinburne: "Even the weariest river winds
somewhere safe to sea."

Meditation and other spiritual disciplines are
largely meant to give us the toughness required
to take hold of our lives. Without this toughness, despite the better goals we may cherish in
our hearts, we will not be able to take the road
that leads where we want to go.

Know the Self as Lord of the chariot,
The body as the chariot itself,
The discriminating intellect as
The charioteer, and the mind as the reins.
The senses, say the wise, are the horses,
Selfish desires are the roads they travel.

KATHA UPANISHAD

The Upanishads say that your body is like a chariot drawn by five powerful horses, the five senses. These horses travel not so much through space as through time. They gallop from birth towards death, pursuing the objects of their desire. The discriminating intellect is the charioteer, whose job it is not to drive you over a cliff. The reins he holds are the mind – your thoughts, emotions, and desires.

This image is packed with implications. For one, the job of the intellect is to see clearly. The job of the mind is to act as reins. When everything is working in harmony, our highest Self makes all the decisions. The intellect conveys these decisions to the mind, and the senses obey the mind. But when the senses are uncontrolled, they immediately take the road they like best: personal satisfactions, mostly pleasure. Then we are not making the decisions; the horses are.

Learn self-conquest, persevere thus for a time, and you will perceive very clearly the advantage which you gain from it. As soon as you apply yourself to orison, you will at once feel your senses gather themselves together: they seem like bees which return to the hive and there shut themselves up to work at the making of honey. . . . God thus rewards the violence which your soul has been doing to itself. . . . At the first call of the will, they (the senses) come back more and more quickly. At last, after countless exercises of this kind, God disposes them to a state of utter rest and of perfect contemplation.

SAINT TERESA OF AVILA

Complete concentration is complete relaxation. The ability to work on a job with total concentration, and then put it out of your mind when necessary, is a skill which can be cultivated. Through practice, we can learn to drop whatever we are doing, and turn our attention to a more urgent need. When you are absorbed in a favorite book and your partner interrupts you, set the book aside and give your complete attention to what he or she is saying. If part of your mind is on the conversation and part on what you have been reading, there will be division and tension in the mind.

When we practice this one-pointedness during the day, it will greatly help our meditation. The mind will much more quickly become recollected.

God is infinite and without end, but the
soul's desire is an abyss which cannot be filled
except by a Good which is infinite; and the
more ardently the soul longeth after God, the
more she wills to long after him; for God is a
Good without drawback, and a well of
living water without bottom, and the soul is
made in the image of God, and therefore it is
created to know and love God.

JOHANNES TAULER

When human beings reach a state in which their physical wants are more than satisfied, when the optimum level of material abundance and physical comfort is reached, something in us feels a sense of satiation akin to nausea. Absorbed up to then in the pursuit of prosperity and material security, we begin to feel restless, dissatisfied with the limits of life as it is being lived, constrained by the lack of challenges – and of love.

Then it becomes possible to hear a still, small voice speaking from deep below the conscious level of our mind, from beneath the level of conditioned desires. The voice was always there, but we were so busy with other things that we did not hear it. "I want an earth that is healthy, a world at peace, and a heart filled with love," it is saying, "I want my life to count."

Who can map out the various forces at play in one soul? Man is a great depth, O Lord. The hairs of his head are easier by far to count than his feelings, the movements of his heart.

SAINT AUGUSTINE

Most of us never really see the people we live with. Our boyfriend may be right before our eyes, but we do not see him. We see our idea of him, a little model we have made in our mind, and on that we pronounce our judgments.

That is why, when we quarrel with someone, the worst thing we can do is to avoid him or her. We are trying to avoid an image in our own mind, which cannot be done. The mind takes some exaggerated impressions, memories, hopes, and insecurities, draws a quick caricature like one of those sidewalk cartoonists, and then turns up its nose. The person in question should retort, "That's not me; that's your caricature of me. If you don't like it, you don't like your own mind."

To heal our relationships, we have to move closer to people we do not like, learn to work with them without friction. When we do this, we are remaking the images in our mind – which means we are literally remaking the world in which we live.

Offer unto me that which is very dear to thee – which thou holdest most covetable. Infinite are the results of such an offering.

SRI KRISHNA (BHAGAVATAM)

Breaking through to a deeper level of consciousness in meditation is very much like trying to open a door which keeps banging shut. We can get through that door by defying self-will that shows up in the form of strong selfish desires. It may be a craving for cigarettes, or for alcohol, or for some selfish activity that benefits no one – whatever it is, large or small, power is locked up in that desire.

Desire *is* will. Every strong desire has a great deal of will locked up in it; the problem is that usually we do not have any control over it. In a compulsive desire, all that will goes into satisfying *only* that desire. Every time you can turn against a strong desire, therefore, it immediately strengthens your will.

Often you can see the results the very next time you sit down for meditation. You will also find your physical and emotional health improving, your relationships deepening, and your energy increasing. These are signs that you are going forward. The desire to go against selfish desires is the surest sign of grace.

The self-existent Lord pierced the senses
To turn outward. Thus we look to the world
Outside and see not the Self within us.
A sage withdrew his senses from the world
Of change and, seeking immortality,
Looked within and beheld the deathless Self.

KATHA UPANISHAD

Consciousness can be thought of as a kind of elastic modeling clay. Originally pure and shapeless, it takes on the form of individual containers like you and me. Then this clay of consciousness begins to flow out through the senses, following desire; it goes where our attention goes.

When you are listening, for example, to your favorite rock group in stereophonic sound, consciousness-clay runs out of the mind and into the ear. It is difficult to get it back in again. As consciousness is flowing out, vital energy is being lost. That is why people who get conditioned to loud, agitating music usually find their security falling and their restlessness swelling.

In reaching out through the senses, we travel far away from the indivisible unity of life at the center of our being. Physical urges and emotional cravings are powerful forces that fling consciousness away from its center. To live a balanced life, we must be able to flow outwards when necessary, and to center inwards when necessary.

*Then did he see and hear that which no
tongue can express, yet he had of it a joy such
as he might have known in the seeing of the
shapes and substances of all joyous things.
. . . He could do naught but contemplate this
shining brightness; and he altogether forgot
himself and all other things. . . .Then he
said, "If that which I see and feel be not the
kingdom of heaven, I know not what it can
be: for it is very sure that the endurance of all
possible pains were but a poor price to pay for
the eternal possession of so great a joy."*

HEINRICH SUSO

In the later stages of meditation, experiences
may come which deepen our ardent desire to
reach the goal. The annals of mysticism provide
countless examples of these brief glimpses of
the goal. Here is the testimony of Suso, a four-
teenth-century German mystic who speaks of
himself in the third person. While he was alone
in a church with many troubles weighing heavily
on his heart, he was suddenly plunged into absorption so deep that he forgot himself completely.

The last sentence is the key. Whether romantic or spiritual, love does not barter. If we knew
at the outset how much joy there is in the unitive
state, we would cast away all our selfish attachments without hesitation. But in that case it
would not be love of God; it would be a business
transaction. Just as in love, you cannot set conditions in the spiritual quest. You cannot ask the
price. Otherwise these experiences cannot
come.

By the will art thou lost,
by the will art thou found.
By the will art thou free,
captive, and bound.

ANGELUS SILESIUS

In the last stages of the spiritual journey, we are trying to keep consciousness in a continuous, unbroken channel. The morning and evening periods of meditation set the standard; then we try to extend these periods of one-pointed attention through the rest of the day. Attention must become one smooth-flowing stream from morning to night and through the night until morning again. In a sense, it is like taking two ends of consciousness and trying to bring them together into a closed circle.

As the ends of the circle get closer, it is like trying to close floodgates against a powerful river. A student of physics will tell you that the smaller the opening across a river, the faster the water flows through. It is the same in consciousness. All the thoughts that could not get our attention while we were meditating or repeating the mantram, all twenty-four hours worth of them, are just waiting to rush in if we give them an opening.

To everyone this test must come. As long as we repeat the mantram, the distractions will not be able to rush in and flood our consciousness. At that time, after years of training, our will has become an invincible ally, ready to take on the almost superhuman challenge of stilling the mind.

A man once asked the mystic Bayazid:
Who is the true Prince? / The man who
cannot choose, said Bayazid: the man for
whom God's choice is the only possible choice.

BAYAZID AL-BISTAMI

The Lord is extending the gift of immortality to each of us, but we do not reach out to take it because we are holding a few pennies in our hands. I don't know if you have seen infants in this dilemma; it happens at a particular stage of development, when they have learned to grasp but not quite mastered letting go. They have a rattle in one hand; you offer them a toothbrush, and for a while they just look back and forth at the toothbrush, then the rattle, then the toothbrush again. You can almost see the gray matter working: "I want that toothbrush, but how can I take it? My hand is already full."

Similarly, all of us look at the Lord's gift for a long while, asking "What *is* this? How do I know it's real? Give it to me first; then I'll let the pennies go." The Lord smiles and waits. He can offer the gift, but for us to take it, we have to open our hands. And there comes a time when we want something more than pennies so passionately that we no longer care what it costs. Then we open our hands, and discover that for the pennies we have dropped, we have received an incomparable treasure.

*Let no one believe that he has received
the divine kiss, if he knows the truth without
loving it or loves it without understanding it.
But blessed is that kiss whereby not only
is God recognized but also the Father
is loved; for there is never full
knowledge without perfect love.*

SAINT BERNARD

If I haven't come to have faith in the Lord within, who is my real Self, how can I be secure? How can I be at peace? How can I live for others? By "faith" I do not mean mere blind faith, but a deep belief based on personal experience.

It is not enough to have blind faith in spiritual ideals, based on the testimony of the scriptures or spiritual teachers. We must realize these truths for ourselves, in our own life and consciousness. As the Buddha was fond of saying, the spiritual teacher only points the way; we must do our own traveling. The personal example of others may plant the seed in our hearts, inspiring us to meditate, but faith can develop fully only when we begin to reap the benefits of meditation in our own lives.

*Knowing that his past actions may try
to overwhelm him, the devotee must be
prepared to combat them. God will give
him the strength: His Name will be
an impenetrable armor. It will save
him from all the consequences.*

SWAMI BRAHMANANDA

In principle, the training of attention is simple:
when the mind wanders, bring it back to what it
should be doing. The problem arises when the
distraction is not a stray thought, but a compulsive resentment, irritation, apprehension, or
craving. The power of such thoughts is that
there is nothing the ego likes to do more than to
think about itself, and when a self-centered
thought comes up, everything in our conditioning screams, "Hey, look at that! Pay attention to
that!"

Here again, our greatest ally is the mantram.
Whenever a selfish, destructive thought comes
up, repeat the mantram. When the mantram
takes hold, the connection between the thought
and your attention is broken. A compulsive
thought, whether it is anger or depression or a
powerful sense-craving, does not really have
any power of its own. All the power is in the attention we give – and when we can withdraw
our attention, the thought or desire will be helpless to compel us into action.

*Entered into Divine Mind, herself
made over to That, she (the soul) at first
contemplates that Realm, but once she sees
that Higher still she leaves all else aside.
Thus when a man enters a house rich in
beauty he might gaze about and admire the
varied splendor before the master appears;
but once seeing him he would ignore all
else and look to him alone.*

PLOTINUS

This body is not me. It is the house in which I live. If you say that I am so many inches tall, or that I weigh such and such number of pounds, I will reply, "You are not describing me, you are talking about my address."

Since I don't identify myself with my body, I don't associate other people very much with their physical appearance either. If someone asks me, "How tall is John?" I have to take time to try to picture him, then use a mental tape measure to try to remember his height. When someone asks me how old a person is, it takes a certain amount of effort for me to recall even what decade he or she is in.

The mystics tell us we should be concerned less about these details of packaging and concerned more with the contents. When I look at people, I like to look at their eyes. These are the windows into the Resident: the Lord. Gradually, as we become more and more spiritually aware, we will be looking straight into people's eyes and deep into their souls.

Have thy heart in heaven and thy hands
upon the earth. Ascend in piety and descend
in charity. For this is the Nature of Light
and the way of the children of it.

THOMAS VAUGHAN

When our hands are busy with a worthwhile task, and our minds are busy with the mantram, we won't have much chance to brood on our problems. Selfish cravings will not have a chance to grow.

Selfish desires need a lot of attention to thrive. They are like delicate houseplants, not very hardy. Unless their needs are met precisely, they cannot last long. If we do not water and fertilize them regularly – think about them, dream about them, plan and wish – they will wither and die. To get plants to thrive, it is considered helpful to talk to them in soothing, friendly tones. Selfish desires thrive on talk too; the more we talk about them, the stronger they get.

So whenever you feel driven by a compulsive, destructive urge, don't analyze it; don't talk about it; don't dwell on it. Turn your attention away from it by throwing yourself into work for others. It can starve the desire away.

All human evil comes from this:
a man's being unable to sit still in a room.

BLAISE PASCAL

Unless we train it, the very nature of the mind is to keep on hopping from one thing to another, almost at random.

The mind can be very usefully employed, but it has to be trained for its job. Too much of the time the mind is engaged in negative thinking, either about others or about ourselves – a destructive occupation. Training the mind means establishing and maintaining sound shop standards: good, creative, consistently kind thinking, and no around-the-clock activity, either. When the mind has nothing productive to do, we need to learn how to close up shop and let it rest.

The community of the living
is the carriage of the Lord.

HASIDIC PROVERB

Where there is so little love that the carriage is torn asunder, we must love more, and the less love there is around us, the more we need to love to make up the lack.

A man once came to Rabbi Israel Ba'al Shem and said, "My son is estranged from God; what shall I do?" The Ba'al Shem replied simply, "Love him more."

Love him more. Make his happiness more important than your own. This was my Granny's approach to every problem, and I know of no more effective or artistic or satisfying way to realize the unity of life in the world today. It is an approach to life in which everything blossoms, everything comes to fruition. Where there is love, everything follows. To love *is* to know, *is* to act; all other paths to the Lord are united in the way of love.

Return from existence to nonexistence!
You are seeking the Lord
and you belong to him.
Nonexistence is a place of income;
flee it not! This existence of more and less
is a place of expenditure.

JALALUDDIN RUMI

Every one of us has an enormous internal savings account of vitality. In our youth we have a margin for experimenting with this vital energy account, for learning through trial and error how it works. But after the age of, say, twenty-five, we need to begin to learn how to live on the interest of this account and not consume the principal. We need to be very careful about which desires we pursue, and not waste our energy in resentment or in fear.

Yet grace adds a whole new dimension to this account. The divine core in all of us is the very source of vital energy, and it is infinite. The more we draw on this divine deposit of wealth – so long as we are drawing from it not for ourselves, but in the service of all life – the more it is replenished. And from our end, as conflict and division fade from the mind, there is no reason why any energy should leak out involuntarily. It follows that vitality builds up to an enormous level.

*Lord grant
that I may not so much seek
to be loved as to love.*

SAINT FRANCIS OF ASSISI

Millions of people today suffer from loneliness. Here Saint Francis is saying, "I know the cause of the malady and I know the secret of its complete cure." No matter what the relationship may be, when you look on another person as someone who can give you love, you are really *faking* love. That is the simplest word for it. If you are interested in *making* love, in making it grow without end, try looking on that person as someone you can give your love to – someone to whom you can go on giving always.

Learning to love is like swimming against the current of a powerful river; most of our conditioning is pushing us in the other direction. So it is a question of developing your muscles: the more you use them, the stronger they get. When you put the other person's welfare foremost every day, no matter how strong the opposing tide inside, you discover after a while that you can love a little more today than you did yesterday. Tomorrow you will be able to love a little more still.

*Thou must be emptied of that
wherewith thou art full, that thou mayest be
filled with that whereof thou art empty.*

SAINT AUGUSTINE

In India we have a flaming hot chili pepper called
chinimulaku, "little thing," in my mother
tongue. It is smaller than your little finger, so
small that you don't take it seriously; but even a
tiny bite will burn your mouth. Self-will is like
that; a little dose of it can cause harm for a long
time.

The remedy for self-will, in the Buddha's language, is *nirvana*, from *nir*, "out," plus *vana*,
"to blow." You don't snuff self-will out in one
day; you have to keep blowing away, in meditation and then during the day, especially in your
relationships. This world is a place where we
learn to return goodwill for ill will and love for
hatred, to work harmoniously with others, and
to put other people's welfare before our own.
You keep blowing for years and years and one
day the fire of self-will goes out.

What we hope ever to do with ease,
we must first learn to do with diligence.
SAMUEL JOHNSON

Plain old inertia is the underlying cause of many of our day-to-day difficulties. You will be feeling listless, oppressed, weighted down by lassitude; you won't want to do anything at all. You may feel persecuted: "Why shouldn't I sit around if I feel like it?" You may feel you are not in the best condition physically, with aches and pains that nobody understands except yourself.

To release yourself from this inertia, the first step is physical. The worst thing you can do is rest. Rest is what you have been doing; what is required is to get moving on something. Superficial physical symptoms may come by way of protest: a dull, throbbing headache, nerves on edge, no circulation in your legs, a head as heavy as your heart. Get up and go for a walk – and walk fast, repeating the mantram, even if you don't feel equal to it. Try to walk a little faster than you feel you can.

After ten minutes or so you will find yourself breaking through that physical lethargy. Keep walking, and you will see that the rhythm of your breathing has improved, your spirits are lighter, you are ready to face the next challenge of the day.

*Perseverance is more prevailing than
violence; and many things which cannot be
overcome when they are together, yield
themselves up when taken little by little.*

PLUTARCH

With every thought, we are working on our destiny. When a sculptor creates an elephant, each touch of the chisel shapes the stone. While carving an eye he barely strokes the stone, but those light strokes are as vital as the rough shaping blows. There is no such thing as an unimportant blow.

Similarly, every thought shapes our lives. There is no such thing as a little thought, no such thing as an unimportant thought. It may be heavy, it may be light, but it always should be well directed, with discrimination and precision.

*Mental tensions, frustrations, insecurity,
aimlessness are among the most damaging
stressors, and psychosomatic studies have
shown how often they cause migraine
headache, peptic ulcers, heart attacks,
hypertension, mental disease, suicide,
or just hopeless unhappiness.*

HANS SELYE

A great deal of psychological stress comes from the rush and hurry of a frantic mind, which jumps recklessly to unwarranted conclusions, rushes to judgments, and often is going too fast to see events and people as they truly are. Such a mind keeps the body under continual tension. It is constantly on the move, desiring, worrying, hoping, fearing, planning, defending, rehearsing, criticizing. It cannot stop or rest except in deep sleep, when the whole body, particularly the nervous system, heaves a sigh of great relief and tries to repair the damage of the day.

Simply by slowing down the mind – the first purpose of meditation – much of this tension can be removed. Then we are free to respond to life's difficulties not as sources of stress but as challenges, which will draw out of us deeper resources than we ever suspected we had. A one-pointed mind is slow and sound, which gives it immense resilience under stress. With a mind like this, we always have a choice in how we respond to life around us.

*I went to the woods because I wished to live
deliberately, to front only the essential facts
of life, and see if I could not learn what it had
to teach, and not, when I came to die,
discover that I had not lived.*

HENRY DAVID THOREAU

*The One remains,
the many change and pass;
Heaven's light forever shines,
earth's shadows fly;
Life, like a dome of many-colored glass,
Stains the white radiance of eternity,
Until Death tramples it to fragments.*

PERCY BYSSHE SHELLEY

Everyone will agree that some day the body must grow old, decay, and drop away, but not many will face the fact that it will happen to them. If a person really believes he will die, he will do something about it.

The mystics tell us to live each moment as if it were our last, and the man or woman who repeats the mantram regularly with real devotion is actually preparing for death. The person who has become established in the mantram, who has made the mantram an integral part of his or her consciousness, is prepared for death at all times.

When we realize fully that we are not this changing body but the changeless Self who dwells in the body, we conquer death here and now.

Who is wise? He who learns from all men.

TALMUD, SAYINGS OF THE FATHERS

In many disagreements – not only in the home but even at the international level – it is really not ideological differences that divide people. It is lack of respect, which is another way of saying lack of love. Most disagreements do not even require dialogue; all that is necessary is a set of flash cards. If Romeo wants to make a point with Juliet, he may have elaborate intellectual arguments for buttressing his case, but while his mouth is talking away, his hand just brings out a big card and shows it to Juliet: "I'm right." Then Juliet flashes one of hers: "You're wrong!" You can use the same cards for all occasions, because that is all most quarrels amount to.

What provokes people is not so much facts or opinions, but the arrogance of these flash cards. Kindness here means the generous admission – not only with the tongue but with the heart – that there is something in what you say, just as there is something in what I say. If I can listen to you with respect, it is usually only a short time before you listen with respect to me. Once this attitude is established, most differences can be made up. It may require a lot of hard work, but the problem is no longer insoluble.

If you go on working with the light
available, you will meet your Master,
as he himself will be seeking you.

RAMANA MAHARSHI

The word *guru* has passed into the English language, but it is often misunderstood. *Guru* simply means "heavy," one who is so heavy that he or she can never be shaken. A guru is a person who is so deeply established within himself that no force on earth can affect the complete love he or she feels for everyone. If you curse him, he will bless you; if you harm her, she will serve you; and if you exploit him, he will become your benefactor.

It is good for us to remember that the guru, the spiritual teacher, is in every one of us. The outer teacher makes us aware of the teacher within.

We are told in the Hindu scriptures to select a teacher very carefully. We should not get carried away by personal appearance – because we like his hair style or her robes. There is a good test of authenticity: does their life accord with what they teach? We have to listen carefully, judge carefully, then make our own decision. Once we make a decision and select an outer teacher who is suited to our spiritual needs, we should be prepared to be loyal. To the extent we can be loyal to the outer teacher, we are being loyal to ourselves.

*The measure of your holiness is
proportionate to the goodness of your will.*

JAN VAN RUYSBROECK

The will does not grow weak through neglect.
Rather, we attack it – usually through absurd
little self-indulgences: a bite of this, a drink of
that, an unkind word, an unnecessary com-
plaint. We say, "What does it matter?" What
matters is the strength of our will. Every time we
give in to a self-indulgent impulse, we are twit-
ting the will.

Not content with taunting, we sometimes
stage guerrilla raids: we sneak down to the
refrigerator, say, and drop a slice of pizza and
a beer into our mouths. "After all," we ask,
"who's the wiser?" No one may be the wiser, but
the will is weaker.

The will can withstand a lot of this kind of
abuse, but eventually it may go into hiberna-
tion. Willpower is still there, but it needs to be
roused. We wake up the will by resisting all sorts
of little, self-indulgent desires.

To be right, a person must do one of two things: either he must learn to have God in his work and hold fast to him there, or he must give up his work altogether. Since, however, man cannot live without activities that are both human and various, we must learn to keep God in everything we do, and whatever the job or place, keep on with him, letting nothing stand in our way.

MEISTER ECKHART

We can train our attention wherever we are, whatever we are doing. The benefits are well worth the discipline.

Everybody knows what it is like to share the highway with a bad driver. He is driving along in the lane next to you and suddenly, without warning, he wanders into your lane. Then, with equal abruptness, he realizes what he has done and overreacts – first with the brake, then with the accelerator – and darts back into his own lane. He's an accident waiting to happen.

If we could only see it, everything in life suffers like this when attention wanders. A mind that darts from subject to subject is out of control, and the person who follows its whims weaves through life, running into difficult situations and colliding with other people. But the mind that is steady stays in its own lane. It cannot be swept away by an impulsive desire or fear; it cannot be haunted by an unpleasant memory or by anxiety about the future. There is no skill more worth learning than the art of directing attention as we choose.

Living creatures are nourished by food,
and food is nourished by rain; rain itself is
the water of life, which comes from
selfless worship and service.

SRI KRISHNA (BHAGAVAD GITA)

We have been conditioned to look to food for some kind of deeper fulfillment. Food can entertain us, we are told. It is exciting, romantic, adventurous, exotic. Vast sums of money are spent trying to get us to buy a certain brand of potato chip or to prefer one brand of frozen pizza over another. In the midst of this carnival atmosphere, it is easy to forget that the real purpose of food is to nourish our bodies.

Eating together with those we love, eating nutritious food that has been prepared with love – this *can* nourish our inner needs, as well as our bodies. Taking time at meals to talk to each other and enjoy the meal as a shared sacrament, this is rare today. People are so busy that even meals have become something to be gotten through as quickly as possible. We need to slow down, take the time to prepare nutritious meals and rearrange our schedules so that we can be together.

*We are all dependent on one
another, every soul of us on earth.*

GEORGE BERNARD SHAW

*Nothing hath separated us from God
but our own will, or rather our own will is
our separation from God.*

WILLIAM LAW

To draw closer to others, you have to rebel
against yourself. Often you will have to hurt
your own private feelings so that others can
benefit. "Thy will be done," Jesus says, not "my
will be done." Thy will is unity; my will is separateness. It is so terribly difficult to practice this
that most people do not try; those who do try
often do not persist. But if you have the inner
toughness this fierce fight requires, you will find
you need less and less tape to measure the gap between you and others. Finally you discover you
are at the center, no longer separate from the
whole.

Man is what he believes.

ANTON CHEKHOV

You are what the deep faith of your heart is. If you believe that money is going to make you happy, then you will go after money. If you believe that pleasure will make you happy, you will go after pleasure. Because, "As a man thinketh in his heart, so is he." Not as he thinketh in his head. There is a vast distance from the head to the heart. In the Greek and Russian Orthodox traditions, they say that whatever spiritual knowledge you have in your head must be brought down into your heart. This takes many, many years.

Love all that has been created by God, both
the whole and every grain of sand. Love
every leaf and every ray of light. Love the
beasts and the birds, love the plants, love
every separate fragment. If you love each
separate fragment, you will understand the
mystery of the whole resting in God.

F.M. DOSTOEVSKY

Most of us think of love as a one-to-one relationship, which is the limitation of love on the
physical level. But there is no limit to our capacity to love. We can never be satisfied by loving
just one person here, another there. Our need is
to love completely, universally, without any
reservations – in other words, to become love
itself.

Abide in peace, banish cares,
take no account of all that happens,
and you will serve God according to
His good pleasure, and rest in Him.

SAINT JOHN OF THE CROSS

We have many stories from the Hindu scriptures about gambling, some about kings who lost entire kingdoms gambling at dice. There is the moving story of King Yudhishthira, who lost his kingdom and went into exile, and yet came back, after a terrible battle, to regain everything through the grace of Sri Krishna.

Many people are tempted to gamble, to take risks, when the stakes are high. The mystics would ask us, "Why don't you bet on goodness? Try to be kind to someone who is unkind to you, and look upon it as a gamble."

Of course we are not sure how the other person is going to respond – that is the thrill of it. If they add insult to injury, why not double your bet? Isn't that what people do at roulette? You just keep on doubling your bet until one day you redeem all your losses.

It may not work at the casino, but in life this is the only strategy that pays in the end. After all, what every one of us is trying to do is break into the bank inside, to get our hands on the real treasures of life – rich relationships and resources for contributing to the happiness of all. This is what everybody wants, and to get it we have to gamble on goodness.

Let us not be justices of the peace,
but angels of peace.

SAINT THERESE OF LISIEUX

This kind of response does not come easily. Dealing with acrimonious situations with a calm patience requires toughness as well as love. Sometimes a little creativity helps, too. There is a story about one of Saint Francis of Assisi's earliest disciples, Brother Juniper, that bears this out. Once, when a superior had reprimanded him with great severity, Brother Juniper was so disturbed that he could not sleep. He got up in the middle of the night and prepared some porridge with a big lump of butter on top, and took it to his superior's room. "Father, I have prepared this porridge for you and beg you to eat it." The superior told him to go away and let him sleep. "Well," said Brother Juniper simply, "would you be so kind as to hold the light while I eat it?" The superior laughed in spite of himself, and was sporting enough to sit down with Brother Juniper so they could eat the porridge together.

We may not be so ingenuous as Brother Juniper, but we can still learn to head off resentment in every way possible.

Those who eat too much or eat too little,
who sleep too much or sleep too little,
will not succeed in meditation. But those
who are temperate in eating and sleeping,
work and recreation, will come to the end
of sorrow through meditation.

SRI KRISHNA (BHAGAVAD GITA)

Once, when the Buddha was told that one of his disciples was having trouble, he went to the young man's room to see what the problem was. This young man had been born in a rich family, and he had been trained in music, so he still kept his *vina* in the corner of his room. When the Buddha entered, he saw the vina and said, "Let me see if I can play your vina."

The disciple reluctantly brought it forward. He didn't know that the Buddha had been an expert musician.

The Buddha tightened the strings of the vina until they were about to break. The disciple protested, "You are not supposed to tighten the strings like that, Blessed One, they will break!"

So the Buddha, with tender cunning said, "Oh, yes! Then should I make them loose?" And he loosened all the strings until they couldn't be played at all.

"Here, let me do it for you, Blessed One," said the disciple, and he adjusted them. "They are now just right, neither too tight nor too loose."

The Buddha smiled, "Yes, you see, that is what my path is: just right, neither too tight nor too loose. Moderation in everything. Temperance in everything."

Oh! the charm of the Name! It brings light where there is darkness, happiness where there is misery, contentment where there is dissatisfaction, bliss where there is pain, order where there is chaos, life where there is death, heaven where there is hell, God where there is Maya. He who takes refuge in that glorious Name knows no pain, no sorrow, no care, no misery. He lives in perfect Peace.

SWAMI RAMDAS

Repeating the Holy Name is a powerful way to harness a very natural tendency of the human mind: to brood. Every compulsion gets its grip from this tendency. The mind takes a trifling remark or incident – no bigger than a limp balloon – and starts to inflate it by thinking about it over and over and over, blowing it up until it fills your consciousness. You can't think about anything else.

When the mind starts this blowup routine, the Holy Name restores your perspective by letting out the air. Every time the mind pumps, the Holy Name pricks open a little hole and lets some of your attention get free. The balloon may not collapse immediately – after all, an emotion like anger or desire has powerful lungs. But right from the first, it will not get so obsessively large, which means you have introduced a measure of free choice. Next time the situation comes up, you will find your freedom of choice even greater.

That one I love who is incapable
Of ill will, and returns love for hatred.
Living beyond the reach of I and mine,
And of pain and pleasure, full of mercy,
Contented, self-controlled, of firm resolve,
With all his heart and all his mind given
to Me – with such a one I am in love.

SRI KRISHNA (BHAGAVAD GITA)

In personal relationships, we all get troubled when we do our best to be kind to someone and that person treats us with hostility or ill will in return. This is common in life today, and most of us quickly reach the end of our tether. "I don't want to see you again," we say. "I want to get as far away from you as possible!"

All of us have these human impulses. But that is just where the Gita or Jesus or the Buddha would say, "No. That is the way of the timid. That is the way of the weak." Stick it out: not by becoming a doormat, not by blindly obeying whatever command the other person gives you, but by resolutely refusing to hurt anyone no matter how much you have been hurt. It is a great art.

Compassion comes with insight into the heart of life, as we see more clearly the unseen forces that drive a person into action. Ultimately, compassion extends to every creature.

Dive deep, O mind, dive deep
In the ocean of God's beauty;
If you descend to the uttermost depths,
There you will find the gem of love.

BENGALI HYMN

Don't think the purpose of meditation is to go deep into consciousness, wrap a blanket around yourself, and say, "How cozy! I'm going to curl up in here by myself; let the world burn." Not at all. We go deep into meditation so that we can reach out farther and farther to the world outside.

In meditation we are going deep into ourselves, into the utter solitude that is within. As a counterbalance to this, it is necessary to be with people: to laugh with them, to sing with them, and to enjoy the healthy activities of life. It is not a luxury on the spiritual path to have hard work, or to have the company of spiritually oriented people; these are necessary for our spiritual development.

Meditation and selfless action go hand in hand. When we try to live more for others than for ourselves, this will deepen our meditation. When we deepen our meditation, more and more energy will be released with which we can love and help others.

A desire arises in the mind. It is satisfied;
immediately another comes. In the interval
which separates two desires a perfect calm
reigns in the mind. It is at this moment
freed from all thought, love or hate.
Complete peace equally reigns
between two mental waves.

SWAMI SIVANANDA

Through meditation and the enthusiastic obser-
vance of disciplines such as slowing down and
keeping the mind one-pointed, we can learn to
do something that sounds impossible: when
thoughts are tailgating each other, we can slip
into the flow of mental traffic, separate thoughts
that have locked bumpers, and slowly squeeze
ourselves in between.

It sounds terribly daring – the kind of stunt
for which professionals in the movies are paid in
four figures. Yet most of us critically underesti-
mate our strength. We can learn to step right in
front of onrushing emotional impulses such as
fury and little by little, inch by hard-won inch,
start pushing them apart. This takes a lot of solid
muscle in the form of willpower; but just as with
muscles, we can build up willpower with good,
old-fashioned practice.

Once you can do this you will find that there
is not the slightest connection between another
person's provocation and your response. There
seemed to be a connection because your percep-
tions were crowding together. Now that those
thoughts have been separated – even for a hair's
breadth – your response has lost its compulsive
force.

*As a person abandons worn-out clothes
and acquires new ones, so when the body
is worn out a new one is acquired by
the Self, who lives within.*

SRI KRISHNA (BHAGAVAD GITA)

*All that live must die,
Passing through nature to eternity.*

WILLIAM SHAKESPEARE

As a traditional Hindu, my grandmother believed in transmigration, or reincarnation. For her, death was not a painful topic because she believed so firmly that our real Self cannot die. Even though we cannot but grieve when our dear ones pass away, mystics of all religions tell us that underneath this grief we should always remember that death is only a change of rooms.

Whether we believe in one life or in a million lives, the basis of meditation remains valid for all of us. Trying to speculate about previous or future lives serves no practical purpose, since this life is headache enough. Let us confine our attention to this life and try as far as our capacity goes to learn to love here and now.

*Speak when you are angry and you will
make the best speech you will ever regret.*

AMBROSE BIERCE

When we get tense, it is easiest to vent our frustration by making cracks at our children, our wife, or our husband – it is a simple matter of geographic proximity. When we attack other people, when we become a source of trouble to others, it is not because we want to add to their trouble; we have just become an object of trouble to ourselves. When we are agitated, when we are ready to burst our anger upon others, the immediate solution is to go for a long walk, or run, repeating the Holy Name.

In the ultimate analysis, our resentments and hostilities are not against others. They are against our own alienation from our native state, which is cosmic consciousness, Christ-consciousness, Krishna-consciousness. All the time we are being nudged by some latent force within us, trying to remind us what our native state is. Our senses are turned outwards, and we are adepts at personal profit and pleasure, so we do not like to hear these little reminders; but the needling goes on.

*They are not following dharma who resort to
violence to achieve their purpose. But those
who lead others through nonviolent means,
knowing right and wrong, may be called
guardians of the dharma.*

THE BUDDHA

The Hindu and Buddhist scriptures often use
the word *dharma*, which comes from a root
meaning "to support." It is a very difficult word
to translate into English. In fact, there is really
no English equivalent, but dharma is that which
supports us, keeps us together. Dharma is the
central law of our being, which is to extinguish
our separateness and attain Self-realization, to
lose ourselves and be united with the Lord. This
is the universal law inscribed on every cell of our
being, and the proof of it is that the more we live
for others, the healthier our body becomes, the
calmer our mind becomes, the clearer our intellect becomes, the deeper our love and wisdom
become.

The Hindu and Buddhist scriptures also
speak of a personal dharma. This is our present
context, our present assets and liabilities. On the
spiritual path, we start from where we stand.
Later on, as our capacities grow, our opportunities for service will become greater. What is the
right occupation now may not be right later on,
but as long as it is not at the expense of others,
our job can be made a part of our spiritual journey.

By love may He be gotten and holden,
by thought never.

THE CLOUD OF UNKNOWING

The supreme, radiant Being that dwells in our own consciousness cannot be attained by any amount of reasoning, for this Being is one and indivisible, beyond all duality. But by loving Him "with all our heart, and all our soul, and all our strength," we can come to live in Him completely. When we learn to love Her more than we love ourselves, our consciousness is unified.

It is all very well to talk about the Ultimate Reality, the Great Void, but we cannot love a Void. Here it is that we need the Lord in an aspect we can love and understand – the Supreme Poet, the sustainer and protector of all, from whom we came into existence and to whom we shall return. We need a divine ideal like Sri Krishna, Jesus the Christ, the Compassionate Buddha, or the Divine Mother.

There is nothing abstract about this kind of love, nothing philosophical. Loving the Lord means loving the innermost Self in all those around us. We need only somehow to increase our capacity to love. Because we do not live in what we think; we live in what we love.

*All that is sweet, delightful, and amiable in
this world, in the serenity of the air, the
fineness of seasons, the joy of light, the
melody of sounds, the beauty of colours, the
fragrancy of smells, the splendour of precious
stones, is nothing else but Heaven breaking
through the veil of this world, manifesting
itself in such a degree and darting forth in
such variety so much of its own nature.*

WILLIAM LAW

The great Hindu scriptures say that God is absolute truth, absolute joy, absolute beauty. Any scientist who is seeking the absolute truth, as Einstein did, is seeking God. Anyone seeking absolute joy, whether in a tavern or in the shopping mall or in Monte Carlo, is seeking God. And anyone who is seeking absolute beauty – on a canvas or a stage or a mountaintop – is seeking God. What lovers of beauty seek in paintings, in sculpture, in dance, in music is just a reflection of the absolute beauty that is God. The real source of all beauty is God, the Beloved.

So, there is nobody who is not seeking God. The scientist in his lab, the pleasure seeker at the casino, the artist in her studio: all are seeking God. We are all lovers, restlessly searching for the Beloved, hoping to catch a glimpse of the Face behind the veil.

*Being is desirable because it is identical with
Beauty, and Beauty is loved because it is
Being. . . . We ourselves possess Beauty when
we are true to our own being; ugliness is in
going over to another order; knowing
ourselves, we are beautiful; in
self-ignorance, we are ugly.*

PLOTINUS

This morning a friend said to me, "You look good!" I appreciated the compliment, of course, but I also felt a little amused. I almost wanted to reply, "What do you mean? I *am* good." Some people are mostly concerned with looking good. We should not be content with that. If we want a compliment, we should be good; and then others will say, "You are good."

Today, it is said that the image has become the person. If the public relations people can make you look good, you come to believe that you are good.

We should never allow ourselves to emulate or admire images that merely look good. Whether in sports or entertainment or politics, celebrities offer good role models only when they stand for lasting values.

*Lunch kills half of Paris,
supper the other half.*

MONTESQUIEU

I suggest eating moderately. Fasting may not be as easy as feasting, but after a while it is not too different. Both are extremes. It is not hard to go the extreme way, but what is really difficult is neither to fast nor to feast, but to be moderate in everything we do. This is what the Buddha called the Middle Path. It requires great artistry and vigilance. Instead of negating the body and senses, we train them to be valuable instruments.

I try to eat good, wholesome food in temperate quantities in order to strengthen the body. If my body is not strong, I cannot contribute to the welfare of society, and I cannot give the best account of myself in life. We harness our physical, mental, and intellectual capacities not to make money or achieve power or fame, but to use these faculties to make our contribution to life.

Ask, and it shall be given you;
seek, and ye shall find;
knock, and it shall be opened unto you.

THE GOSPEL ACCORDING TO
SAINT MATTHEW

Most of us have not tried knocking on the door that Jesus is talking about. We are content to spend all our time exploring the outside of the house. The lawn, the shrubs, the trellis and the porch swing receive all our attention, so that we never even get inside, never seek out the One who is waiting there. We turn our cottage into House Beautiful, paint it and repaint it, but never so much as knock on the door.

Not only are we not looking for anybody inside, we are convinced that no one is there. If there is a God, we think he is surely outside, as is everything else that catches our attention. Vaguely, fondly even, we may sometimes imagine as we go about our business that Someone is probably keeping an eye on us. But if we will open our ears, we can hear the murmurings from within, the faint stir and rustle of a presence deep inside of us, and a voice hauntingly beautiful. Once we hear that, we will pound on the door with all our might, so that we can enter and meet the One who has been waiting so long.

*I reached in experience the Nirvana which is
unborn, unrivalled, secure from attachment,
undecaying and unstained. This condition is
indeed reached by me which is deep, difficult
to see, difficult to understand, tranquil,
excellent, beyond the reach of mere logic,
subtle, and to be realized only by the wise.*

THE BUDDHA, ON ATTAINING
ENLIGHTENMENT

The Buddha is sometimes quoted as saying that
desire is suffering. A more accurate translation is
that *selfish* desire is suffering – in fact, the source
of all suffering. But desire itself is simply power,
neither good nor bad.

Without the tremendous power of desire,
there can be no progress on the spiritual path;
there can be no progress anywhere. The whole
secret of spiritual transformation is turning
selfish desire into selfless desire, transforming
personal passions into the overwhelming desire
to attain life's highest goal. This is not repression; it is transformation.

*When the senses contact sense objects, a
person experiences cold or heat, pleasure or
pain. These experiences are fleeting; they
come and go. Bear them patiently.*

SRI KRISHNA (BHAGAVAD GITA)

*An Englishman thinks he is moral
when he is only uncomfortable.*

GEORGE BERNARD SHAW

The Gita does not say that we should not go
after pleasure. When I first heard this from my
grandmother, I really took to the Gita immediately; but I wasn't expecting what she said next:
"The Gita doesn't say not to go after pleasure; it
says that when you go after pleasure you are also
going after pain."

It is not possible for most of us to accept this.
We are always cherishing the distant hope that
while no other human being has ever succeeded
in isolating pleasure, *we* are going to perform
this miraculous operation and then live in a state
of pleasure always. To enter a state of abiding joy
we must sometimes say no to pleasure while ac-
cepting pain with a smile.

Just as we should not pursue pleasure, we
should not pursue pain, either. Pleasure and
pain form a single duality of experience. We
must learn to remain calm in both, not clinging
to either.

When the soul is naughted and transformed,
then of herself she neither works nor
speaks nor wills, nor feels nor hears nor
understands; neither has she of herself the
feeling of outward or inward, where she may
move. And in all things it is God who rules
and guides her, without the mediation of any
creature. And the state of this soul is then a
feeling of such utter peace and tranquillity
that it seems to her that her heart, and her
bodily being, and all both within and
without, is immersed in an ocean of utmost
peace. . . . And she is so full of peace that
though she press her flesh, her nerves,
her bones, no other thing comes forth
from them than peace.

SAINT CATHERINE OF GENOA

When everything you do is to please the Lord, your life is very simple. It is not that you don't face complicated problems; every day life is likely to bring challenges, but you have learned to face them without inner turmoil. All you do is ask what would please your Lord. You are no longer interested in pleasing yourself or in pleasing anybody else in particular; you want only to please God.

Putting others first is an area in which the mind can often play tricks on us. Interestingly enough, often when we believe we are thinking of others and putting their needs first, we are really just trying to please – which means we are really thinking about ourselves. When we truly are putting others first, we cannot but feel at peace with ourselves.

*Ahimsa is the attribute of the soul, and
therefore, to be practiced by everybody in all
affairs of life. If it cannot be practiced in all
departments, it has no practical value*

MAHATMA GANDHI

A*himsa* is usually translated as "nonviolence,"
but this is misleading and falls far short of the real
significance of the word. When all violence has
subsided in my heart, my native state is love. I
would add that even avoiding a person we dislike
can be a subtle form of *himsa* or violence. Therefore, in everyday terms, ahimsa often means
bearing with difficult people.

In Kerala we have a giant, fierce-looking
plant called elephant nettle. You have only to
walk by for it to stretch out and sting you. By the
time you get home, you have a blister that won't
let you think about anything else. My grandmother used to say, "A self-willed person is like
an elephant nettle."

That is why the moment we see somebody
who is given to saying unkind things, we make a
detour. We pretend we have suddenly remem-
bered something that takes us in another direction, but the fact is that we just don't want to be
stung. Whenever I complained of a classmate I
did not like, my granny would say, "Here, you
have to learn to grow. Go near him. Let yourself
slowly get comfortable around him; then give
him your sympathy and help take the sting out
of his nettleness."

*For now we see through a glass darkly; but
then face to face; now I know in part; but
then shall I know even as also I am known.*

I CORINTHIANS

In moments of trouble we are seeing "through a
glass darkly," as Paul puts it, often through the
distorting medium of personal grievances. Instead of lashing back or sulking in our tent like
Achilles, we can repeat the Holy Name to clear
our eyes.

In times of distress, when you try to call up
the mantram or Holy Name, you may have
difficulty even locating it. Your attention will be
caught in your own turmoil, and every time you
draw it toward God, it will rebel and slip back
again.

Here is where toughness comes in. Simply
bring your attention back to the Holy Name
over and over again until your mind is calm.
Then, when you go back to the scene that
brought you distress, you can stay calm and
compassionate. You can speak kindly, even if
the response is not kind. You are inwardly secure in your love.

*Experience is the name everyone
gives to their mistakes.*

OSCAR WILDE

*He who is not tempted, what does he know?
And he who is not tried, what are
the things he knows?*

ECCLESIASTICUS

Mistakes are a natural part of growing up, and there is no need to brood over them. As my grandmother used to tell the young girls in my ancestral home when they began to work in the kitchen, we can all expect to do a little spilling and burning in order to learn to cook.

Even though we have a certain margin for error, the sooner we can learn from our mistakes, the less suffering we will have to undergo in life. The consequences of a mistake may last for many years, and in making a major decision, many of us are prone to overcalculate the satisfaction we are going to get out of it and overlook the suffering involved for ourselves as well as others. We often forget that the action we are contemplating contains the seed of its result.

For those who wish to climb the mountain
of spiritual awareness, the path is selfless
work. For those who have attained the
summit of union with the Lord,
the path is stillness and peace.

SRI KRISHNA (BHAGAVAD GITA)

In order to climb the Himalayas within us, we have to train ourselves, little by little, day by day. Sir Edmund Hillary, who climbed Mount Everest for the first time, did not just stand at the bottom, take one leap, and land on top. He practiced climbing for a long time to learn all the required skills; and for you and me to climb the spiritual mountain, we, too, have to strengthen our muscles over a long, long period of time.

Most of us get our training experience in the heart of the family. In mountain climbing, you tie yourself to others with ropes and when somebody slips you haul him up and save him. Similarly, in living with family or friends, if somebody slips you do not say, "Aha! Served him right!" You pull him up. And when you slip, she pulls you up. It is a loving exchange. So there is greater safety when people live together and help one another.

Do not be dismayed, daughters, at the number of things which you have to consider before setting out on this Divine journey, which is the royal road to Heaven. By taking this road we gain such precious treasures that it is no wonder if the cost seems to us a high one. The time will come when we shall realize that all we have paid has been nothing at all by comparison with the greatness of our prize.

SAINT TERESA OF AVILA

Meditation may require a lifetime to master, but it will have been a lifetime well spent. Those who offer instant enlightenment mislead us. After all, we have to bring the mind itself under control, and there is no more difficult task in life. We should be prepared for a lifetime of challenge. But then, we need challenges, or we stagnate.

If you want to judge your progress, ask yourself these questions: Am I more loving? Is my judgment sounder? Do I have more energy? Can my mind remain calm under provocation? Am I free from the conditioning of anger, fear, and greed?

Spiritual awareness reveals itself as eloquently in character development and selfless action as in mystical states. Authentic mystical experience changes the way you see the world and the way you live.

Heaven lies about us in our infancy.

WILLIAM WORDSWORTH

*Except ye be converted, and become as
little children, ye shall not enter
into the kingdom of heaven.*

THE GOSPEL ACCORDING TO
SAINT MATTHEW

In India, stories about Sri Krishna as a little boy remind us of the divinity of children. In one such story, Krishna's mother, Yashoda, was churning curds to make butter in an earthen pot, using a wooden pestle which she moved round and round by means of a rope. Little Krishna was playing nearby but, as usual, he was soon up to mischief.

When his mother tried to get him to obey her, he was defiant. She took the rope she was using and said, "If you don't stop your mischief, I'm going to tie you up." Little Krishna silently put out his arms.

Yashoda tried to tie his hands, but the rope would not reach around his wrists. She got another rope. It, too, was not long enough. Soon everybody on the street had become interested. They all brought ropes and tied them together until the rope was very, very long, yet it would still not reach because of the infinity of the Lord present in baby Krishna. How could anyone tie up those slender hands that held the whole cosmos?

Consciousness of the divinity of children can inspire parents – and all caring adults – to lead more selfless lives.

*It is a funny thing about life; if you
refuse to accept anything but the best
you very often get it.*

SOMERSET MAUGHAM

We must be careful not to mistake agitation for fulfillment, excitement for joy. When our mind is not turbulent for a while, we tend to think we're in a slump and start groping about for something that can stir it up again: a cup of coffee, a thrill-packed movie, a stiff drink, a drug, a spirited quarrel, anything to "get the juices flowing." Taken one by one these may seem like innocuous forms of indulgence, yet in their long-range cumulative impact, they deplete us and deflect us from our real goals.

When we fix our eyes on a higher goal, we begin to see beyond the immediate appeal of short-term satisfactions. Confident that a far greater joy is ours, we can hold out against the voices from all sides that cajole, "Eat this; drink that; watch this; buy that." True joy is found when the mind is still, not when it is excited.

There has never been a time when you and I
have not existed, nor will there be a time
when we will cease to exist. As the same
person inhabits the body through childhood,
youth, and old age, so too at the time of death
he attains another body. The wise are not
deluded by these changes.

SRI KRISHNA (BHAGAVAD GITA)

In our modern civilization we try to cling to time as it rushes past, almost begging time to stop. We want to continue to be what we are now. We don't want to be subjected to the ruthless physical changes that are an inescapable part of life. Yet it is the nature of the body to change, up to the last change we call death. Anybody who tries to cling to what is changing cannot help feeling insecure.

Yet we needn't be helplessly caught in time. There are a number of very simple steps we can take to begin to free ourselves. One of the easiest is to get up early in the morning. This gives you the opportunity to start the day with a leisurely pace – to take a short walk, if you like, and then to have your meditation, without worrying about catching the bus or being on time for school. In meditation, do not be aware of time. There is no need to check the clock; you can learn to time the length of the meditation fairly well by the length of the passage you are using. It is these little things, practiced with diligence, that add up to big changes in our lives.

*As iron put into the fire loseth its rust and
becometh clearly red-hot, so he that wholly
turneth himself unto God puts off all
slothfulness, and is transformed
into a new man.*

THOMAS A KEMPIS

We are made in the image of God. The image is
there, but we need to put in the work to reveal it.
Whenever I hear someone say, "This is just the
way I am; you've got to learn to live with it," I
want to grab him by the collar and plead, "Don't
ever say that!" The miracle of human existence is
that we can change. Simply by virtue of being
human, we have the capacity to change ourselves completely.

All of us carry a cleansing fire hidden inside. It
may be banked with ashes, cold to the touch, but
a spark of the divine is there nonetheless, ready
to leap into life. It is nothing less than love of
God. Latent in every one of us, it wants only a
little encouragement before it flares to vibrant
life, burning up everything selfish and impure.
Once ignited and coaxed with the fuel of love for
others, it sheds light and warmth all around.

A soft answer turneth away wrath.
PROVERBS

When you feel angry towards someone, and want to say something unkind, that is all the more reason to speak kindly. If someone provokes you and you respond with anger, you are reinforcing anger as a part of your personality.

So returning kindness for unkindness is not simply being kind to that particular person. You're being kinder to yourself, because you are undoing a compulsion, taking one more step towards being free. You are turning wrath away from yourself, as well as being kind to the other person.

The deconditioning process is straightforward enough: when anger comes up, don't act on it. When it tries to tell you what to do, say no. Repeat the mantram, go out for a long, brisk walk if possible, and throw yourself into hard, concentrated work, preferably for the benefit of others. When you can shift your attention to your work or to the mantram, you have shifted it away from the anger. Immediately the anger-tendency is weakened a little.

*It is great wisdom to know how to be silent
and to look at neither the remarks, nor the
deeds, nor the lives of others.*

SAINT JOHN OF THE CROSS

Most of us cannot help comparing ourselves
with others, at least now and then. In fact, this
has become so entrenched today that in order to
have self-esteem, it seems almost necessary to
say, "I am better than he, so I am good." As long
as we compete with each other and compare one
with another, a certain amount of envy is inescapable. It is the very rare person who is completely free from jealousy.

But as our spiritual awareness grows, we will
know that the Lord is present in everyone and
that there is a uniqueness about everyone. The
truly spiritual person never tries to compare
himself with others, or others among themselves. I have never been able to understand the
compelling phrase, "keeping up with the
Joneses." It does not matter very much whether
we keep up with Tom Jones or anybody else;
what is important is for us to keep up with the
Lord by serving him in everyone around us.

We can keep this ideal before our eyes, by not
comparing ourselves with others, remembering
that all of us have complete worth and value because the Lord is present in us all the time.

*My mind withdrew its thoughts from
experience, extracting itself from the
contradictory throng of sensuous images,
that it might find out what that light was
wherein it was bathed. . . . And thus, with
the flash of one hurried glance, it attained to
the vision of That Which Is.*

SAINT AUGUSTINE

Even when we are not speaking or acting, most
of us find that our mind still goes on working –
thinking, daydreaming, planning, worrying,
eating up precious energy that should be going
to the body to maintain health. In a sense, our
mind is in overdrive all the time. But when we
have learned to meditate, we can actually shift
the mind out of overdrive and down into fourth
gear, then to third, to second, and eventually to
first. We may even learn how to put our mind
into neutral and park it for a while by the side of
the road.

When we can do that, a much higher faculty –
which the Hindu and Buddhist mystics call
prajna, "wisdom," – comes into play. Then we
will find that we see deep into the heart of life,
with fathomless patience at our disposal. When
we have learned to park the mind even for a short
period, so much vitality is conserved that every
major system in the body gets a fresh lease on
life.

Hasten slowly and ye shall soon arrive.

MILAREPA

Some people are fortunate enough to have a great wealth of vitality. But when we are feeling especially full of energy, we may be likely to take up too many activities at the same time. We make big plans, but then a great deal of our enthusiasm simply drains away in excitement. When we start to put our plans into action, we find we have run out of steam.

The culprit here is the excitement itself. It is the nature of excitement that it cannot last. It has to die down, and when it does, the same project we began with such enthusiasm looks utterly boring. It is full of dull, drab details that we had not foreseen. And we give up. The project has not changed; our energy that fueled it is depleted.

To achieve our highest potential in life, we must cultivate the capacity to carry through. Activity is not achievement. It is not enough to rush about beginning a lot of things and keeping busy. A well-spent life is one that rounds out what it has begun. The life of a great artist or scientist is usually shaped by a single desire, carried through to the very end.

Direct your life to the overriding spiritual goal, and lesser activities will take their proper place.

He who binds to himself a joy
Doth the winged life destroy.
But he who kisses the joy as it flies
Lives in Eternity's sunrise.

WILLIAM BLAKE

One particularly painful compulsion in personal relationships is clutching at our partner or friends for security. This leads to all kinds of trouble. When we grasp at another person, the real tragedy is that we cease to see that person; in our insecurity, he or she becomes merely an object for propping ourselves up. This is an open invitation to jealousy – we see him or her as a character in *our* drama, not in anyone else's – and finally a broken relationship. People may hop from one relationship to another, always grasping and always missing what they are grasping for.

Real love is the result of a lot of hard work over a long period of time. It is developed through trust and loyalty and patience, learning not to say a harsh word or even show disrespect when we are provoked. Over many years this kind of love can grow to such an extent that those you love will *know* you're incapable of hurting them. Imagine the security this brings! Both to you and to them. Your trust and loyalty can be anchored so deep that you never even have a divisive thought.

It is permissible to take life's blessings with both hands provided thou dost know thyself prepared in the opposite event to take them just as gladly. This applies to food and friends and kindred, to anything God gives and takes away. . . . As long as God is satisfied do thou rest content. If he is pleased to want something else of thee, still rest content.

MEISTER ECKHART

In order to live in freedom, we must learn to accept a temporary disappointment, if necessary, when it is for our permanent well-being. Sometimes, when we want to eat a particular dainty that appeals to us, or when we want to eat a little more than is necessary, we can't help feeling a tug at the heart as we push away from the table. We cannot help thinking that we could as well have stayed on for five more minutes of pleasure, forgetting that it would probably be followed by five hours of stomachache at night. The right time to get up from the meal is when we want just a little more. This is real artistry, real gourmet judgment: when we find that everything is so good that we would like to have one more helping, we get up and walk away.

*For you the world outside will now stand
transformed as the very expression or
manifestation of God – everywhere the
Light of God will dazzle your eyes; even in
the apparent diversity and activity of nature
you will strangely be conscious of an
all-pervading stillness and peace of the
Eternal – a consciousness which is
unshakably permanent. You will also feel
that you are liberated from the harassing
dualities of life followed by the crowning
experience of an abiding state
of ineffable ecstasy.*

SWAMI RAMDAS

Once, when Krishna was a baby, the women of his village came running to tell his mother, Yashoda, that her little boy was eating sand. Baby Krishna denied everything, shaking his little head with determination. But his mother saw the mischief in his eyes and caught hold of his chin to see for herself.

Krishna obligingly opened his mouth wide. There, within that little rosebud of a mouth, Yashoda saw the vast starry sky with its innumerable worlds, and all the creatures that had ever lived and would ever be born. Yashoda was overcome with fear and wonder, for this was the child she had been scolding and treating like her own. After a moment, the vision faded, but after that Yashoda always knew the secret – Krishna was her beloved little boy, but he was also the Lord of the Universe.

*To the illumined man or woman, a clod of
dirt, a stone, and gold are the same.*

SRI KRISHNA (BHAGAVAD GITA)

Gold is not valuable in itself. It is valuable because there is so little of it. If sand were found
only in small quantities, people would treasure
it in their safe-deposit boxes; they would buy
sand certificates, on important occasions they
would exchange a little sand, and they would
have the expression "as good as sand."

Things cannot give us status. We give status to
things. When Tom gets into his BMW, he is giving status to the car. The car is not giving him status. The car says, "I feel good, because Tom is at
the wheel."

What really gives value to anything is its usefulness in serving others. Our body draws its
value from its usefulness in serving others, and
our life draws its value not from the money we
make, or the prizes we win, or the power we
wield over others, but from the service we give
every day to add a little bit more to the happiness
of our family and our community.

Health, a light body, freedom from cravings,
A glowing skin, sonorous voice, fragrance
Of body: these signs indicate progress
In the practice of meditation.

SHVETASHVATARA UPANISHAD

If you are practicing meditation regularly, be sure to get adequate physical exercise. This is very important. The deeper your interior life, the greater the need for vigorous physical activity. People sometimes fall into a kind of lethargy in the mistaken belief that this is what it means to work without tension. It is just the opposite. The body is our instrument of physical service, and it thrives on vigorous movement. If you are young or already in good condition, "vigorous" here means *vigorous*. Swimming, running, and fast-paced sports that require concentration are all excellent exercise. But unless you are in condition, do not jump into such activities immediately. Work up to them gradually. If you are over thirty-five or have any particular physical problems, ask your doctor to start you on an exercise program.

In meditation we gradually reduce our obsessive identification with the body. The body will begin to feel lighter, our step will be more buoyant, and our senses will come more easily under our control. By getting plenty of physical exercise, we help this process along.

*All this talk and turmoil and noise and
movement and desire is outside of the veil;
within the veil is silence and calm and rest.*

BAYAZID AL-BISTAMI

*There is nothing so lovely and enduring
in the regions which surround us, above
and below, as the lasting peace
of a mind centered in God.*

YOGA VASISHTHA

Steering a middle course between elation and
depression does not mean resigning ourselves to
a flat and monotonous life. Far from it. There is
a third state which is neither elation nor depression, and if we can avoid these two extremes, we
will find the abiding joy which is our real nature.
Most of us have little objection to getting elated,
but none of us are very eager to see depression
setting in. We don't mind being told not to get
depressed, but "Don't let yourself get elated"
sounds puritanical. Yet the time to be cautious is
when the mind is starting to get elated. That is
not the time to pick up the phone and talk and
talk. It is an ideal time to repeat the mantram,
putting to work the energy released in elation.
When you are able to see the specter of depression lurking behind elation and have some personal experience of the joy which transcends
both, you will come to look upon excitement
with a healthy suspicion.

Some people want to see God with their eyes
as they see a cow, and to love Him as they
love their cow – for the milk and cheese and
profit it brings them. This is how it is with
people who love God for the sake of outward
wealth or inward comfort.

MEISTER ECKHART

The external world, so fascinating, so infinite in
its variety, has us firmly in hand and thoroughly
mesmerized. Lasting happiness is almost ours –
over there, just ahead of us, right around the
next corner. When we round that corner and
find it has eluded us, something in us says,
"Keep running! It's just around the *next* corner." Finally, our life becomes a continual pilgrimage around corners. Such is human credu-
lity that even after rounding a thousand corners,
we still say, "The thousand and first, that is *the*
corner."

If we believe that happiness arises only when
some external condition is fulfilled, we consign
ourselves to a perpetual state of discontent. For
even when our expectations are fulfilled, sooner
or later the little voice inside starts again, "More!
More! Now let some other condition be fulfilled!" It is this habit, this almost mechanical
fixation of the mind, that keeps us forever chasing rainbows, until at last we begin to suspect
that the Kingdom of Heaven is within.

*By repeating the name of Krishna or Rama
a man transforms his physical body
into a spiritual body.*

SRI RAMAKRISHNA

In India the mantram *Rama* is called "Rama's arrow." Rama is an incarnation of the Lord, like Krishna, and he was known for his archery; he does all kinds of miraculous things with his bow and his sacred arrows. So the very name of Rama is considered a divine arrow, with which you can shoot down fear, anger, doubt, insecurity, and every other enemy that lurks within.

When I was a boy, a cousin of mine brought home a slingshot. We had never seen one before, so it attracted a good deal of attention. One of my great-uncles got quite curious and demanded, "Let me see." He put a stone in it, pulled it back, and in an instant three or four boys had pounced on him – he was about to shoot the stone straight at his face!

This is suicidal with a slingshot, but not with the arrow of the mantram; inward is just where you do aim it, inward at all that is negative in your consciousness. After a great deal of practice in marksmanship, when a huge fear rises you have the ammunition to shoot it down. When a strong craving comes over you – for smoking, for drink, for drugs – you can take aim and fire.

Grow old along with me!
The best is yet to be,
The last of life, for which the first was made:
Our times are in His hand
Who saith, "A whole I planned,
Youth shows but half; trust God: see all,
nor be afraid!"

ROBERT BROWNING

The body is the temple of the Lord and, if looked after with care, is beautiful even in old age. Childhood has one kind of beauty; youth another; and old age its own special beauty. Even in the evening of her life, my grandmother had a beautiful, healthy body because she was always aware that this temple had to be kept in good order, swept with the mantram broom, and purified through the daily practice of meditation.

We show respect for the Lord within by keeping the body healthy and beautiful. Where books, movies, televison, and our eating and exercise habits are concerned, we must be vigilant to see we are not indulging the senses at the cost of the health of our body or mind. It is not that we cultivate an ascetic attitude. It is just the opposite. We don't mortify the body, but see that every day it gets what it needs for health, so that it will be a valuable, vital instrument until our last day.

If thou shouldst say, "It is enough, I have reached perfection," all is lost. For it is the function of perfection to make one know one's imperfection.

SAINT AUGUSTINE

Among my acquaintances on the Blue Mountain in South India was a Britisher who had climbed many of the higher peaks of the Himalayas. One day he confided to me the feeling of exhilaration he felt on reaching the summit of Annapurna, and standing there in awe in the eternal snows. "Then," he added, "you know, Old Boy, while I gazed out over that magnificent scene, snow-topped mountains as far as the eye could see, the question just popped into my mind: Which peak will be next?" He just couldn't rest on his laurels; he had to keep climbing. That is what gave meaning to his life.

It is the same in meditation. In the spiritual life we shouldn't look forward to the day when we plant our flag on the mountain peak and then retire to a life of tedious leisure. Every time we reach a peak, we will feel a legitimate sense of satisfaction; but at the same time a new and more glorious mountain will probably be beckoning us from the far horizon. That is the glory of living. That is the joy of the spiritual ascent.

*The earth is the Lord's, and the fullness
thereof; the world, and they
that dwell therein.*

PSALMS

You and I are trustees. Nothing belongs to us personally. The resources of our planet have been entrusted to every one of us together. Like good bank trustees, we are expected not to squander these resources but to invest them wisely for our beneficiaries: the rest of life, especially the generations to come.

The trust includes not only the lives and natural resources of the planet, but our inner resources as well. This has very practical implications. We can lessen our potentially exhausting impact on the earth by simplifying our desires and demands. Simplicity is the key to trusteeship.

*Ahimsa is not a policy for the seizure of
power. It is a way of transforming
relationships so as to bring about a peaceful
transfer of power, effected freely and without
compulsion by all concerned, because all
have come to recognize it as right.*

THOMAS MERTON

Bearing with people is the essence of nonviolence. To do this with a feeling of martyrdom,
however, is not very helpful; we need to bear
with people cheerfully. But this does not mean
making ourselves into a doormat. Many people
suffer from the misguided notion that the spiritual life means saying, "Yes, honey, whatever
you want is okay with me. You say; I do." Letting people take undue advantage of us is not
helpful for them any more than it is for us.

We all know that with a selfish person if we
yield an inch he will ask for a yard. With the
selfish person, therefore, it is often necessary
quietly to say no. Don't accept a situation in
which you are exploited, discriminated against,
or manipulated. This is the great art of nonviolent resistance, where you love the person, you
respect him, but you will not allow him to exploit you, because it is bad for him just as it is bad
for you.

Know One, know all.
KATHA UPANISHAD

To know others, you do not have to go and knock on four billion separate doors. Once you have seen your real Self, you have seen the Self in all. It makes it easy to understand and to forgive, and very difficult to quarrel. All of life springs from the same root. The Self in each of us is one and the same.

For this Self, different names are given in different traditions. Christian mystics call it the Christ within. When a person ceases to identify with his perishable self, they say he has become Christ-conscious. The Hindu mystics speak of Krishna-consciousness, or say that such a person has attained complete freedom from the conditioning of time, space, and circumstance. The Buddhists call the same state *nirvana*, from *nir*, 'out' and *vana*, 'to blow.' The ego has been extinguished; there is no more shadow to be mistaken for the real. But the simplest term of all is *Atman* – the Self within.

The more we have the less we own.

MEISTER ECKHART

We have been ruthlessly conditioned to think we can find fulfillment in possessions: to love things, rather than people. So much so, that when we feel an emptiness in our hearts, we go to shopping centers to fill it up.

I am all for living in reasonable comfort, but when I go to shopping centers, I cannot help getting alarmed. Not at the money that is being wasted – there is enough money in this country to waste. But there isn't enough *will* to waste. There isn't enough *energy* to waste. When we hear of the energy crisis, this is it. All our vitality, energy, drive, being sapped and undermined by the ridiculous propaganda: go after this, go after that, and you'll be happy.

Things are not meant to be loved. They are meant only to be used. People are lovable and loving.

*He is not elated by good fortune or depressed
by bad. His mind is established in God, and
he is free from delusion.*

SRI KRISHNA (BHAGAVAD GITA)

*Quiet minds cannot be perplexed or
frightened, but go on in fortune or
misfortune at their own private pace, like a
clock during a thunderstorm.*

ROBERT LOUIS STEVENSON

When the mind gets agitated, we do not see life
as it truly is, as one. It is the constant agitation
going on in our mind that deludes us into believing that you and I are separate.

The question we may well ask is, "If we are to
have neither pleasure nor pain in life, are we not
likely to become insensitive to the joy of life?"
This doubt arises from a wrong assumption,
that there is only pleasure and pain and nothing
else. Always cutting things up into two classes –
everything must be either this or that – is one of
the fatal weaknesses of the intellect. Because of
this dualistic trap, we find it difficult to understand that the rare person who is able to receive
good fortune without getting excited and bad
fortune without getting depressed, lives in abiding joy.

Love is inseparable from knowledge.
SAINT MACARIUS OF EGYPT

When selfish desire is removed from a relationship, there is no hankering to get anything from the other person. We are free to give, which means we are free to love. Then we can give and support and strengthen without reservation.

Interestingly enough, it is only then that we really see each other clearly. The infatuated mind cannot help caricaturing: it sees only what it wants; then, when the desire passes, it sees only what it does not want. Two people who are really in love do not close their eyes to each other's weaknesses. They support each other in overcoming those weaknesses, so that each helps the other to grow.

*Temperance is love surrendering itself
wholly to Him who is its object; courage is
love bearing all things gladly for the sake of
Him who is its object; justice is love serving
only Him who is its object, and therefore
rightly ruling; prudence is love making
wise distinctions between what hinders
and what helps itself.*

SAINT AUGUSTINE

Love for the Lord is not something that descends miraculously from the skies. It can be fostered and deepened immensely through our own effort. At present, very little of our love may be flowing to the Lord. Most of it is flowing down other channels – towards money, or pleasure, or a new sports car or stereo set. In some cases, our vital capacity has been flowing down these channels for so long that they have been cut very deep. Then, when the time comes to dam them up and divert the love in them to flow towards the Lord, we feel we are standing there throwing pebbles into the Grand Canyon. Don't be depressed by the immensity of the task. Just keep on throwing in the pebbles. They may not seem like much, but after a while they all add up.

Take the problem of overeating. A handful of Brazil nuts may be a small thing, and if eaten once in a while they are not likely to do any harm. But if high-calorie snacks are a habit with us, every time we pass up a snack like Brazil nuts, our will becomes a little stronger because we have thrown one more rock into the canyon.

*If one wants to abide in the thought-free
state, a struggle is inevitable. One must fight
one's way through before regaining one's
original primal state. If one succeeds in the
fight and reaches the goal, the enemy,
namely the thoughts, will all subside
in the Self and disappear entirely.*

RAMANA MAHARSHI

Let me continue the metaphor of filling in the Grand Canyons of craving. When we learn to toss in our little cravings, every rock we throw in will precipitate an avalanche. Soon, before we even realize it, the Grand Canyon of that particular craving may be completely filled in. But there is another very practical suggestion I can make here.

It *is* necessary to dam up the old streams down which our love is flowing, but if we do nothing but block the flow, there is always the danger that the dam may break or the water may simply overflow. So instead of giving all of our attention to throwing rocks, we can do our best throughout the day to dig a new channel straight to the Lord in those around us – by being patient, by being loyal, by always keeping our eyes on their welfare rather than our own. For a long time this new stream may flow with only a trickle, but if we keep trying, it will begin to drain off a little of the love that is now flowing down other channels. Finally it will become so deep that all our desires will be unified in a vast flood of love for the Lord within.

Our life is what our thoughts make it.
MARCUS AURELIUS

When tormented by painful thoughts, many of us have cried out, "If only I could stop thinking!" But we don't know how. The mind has gotten stuck, like a needle on a scratched record. We feel helpless to stop it. All the mind can do is repeat the same thought over and over.

Yesterday a friend was playing a Beatles song, and the words went something like, "I am the egg man, I am the walrus. . . ." "Very good," I said to myself, "this is a song about the unity of life." Then the singer went on, "I am the walrus, the walrus, the walrus, the walrus."

"Julia," I said, "why does he go on like this? Can't he think of anything else?"

Julia laughed. "The needle's stuck," she explained. "Doesn't it sound funny?"

When the mind gets stuck, you need to lift the needle and place it a groove or two ahead so that the song can continue. This is a truly amazing accomplishment. The only way I know how to do it is to meditate regularly and repeat the mantram when compulsive thoughts come.

We have no more right to consume happiness
without producing it than to consume
wealth without producing it.

GEORGE BERNARD SHAW

Shopping for things we do not need, even if it is only window-shopping, wastes a lot of vitality; energy flows out with every little desire. It is a surprising connection, but an extravagant shopper will find it difficult to love. He or she scatters love like largesse all over the department store. We can become bankrupt in love this way.

When it comes to our personal vitality, we have no atoms to split, no windmills to set up, no sun to draw on for an alternative source of energy; we have to conserve what we have and make it last. When we find it difficult to love, we can think of it as a personal energy crisis. By not buying things which are neither necessary nor beneficial, we conserve the precious natural resources of the earth, and we save our personal energy, too.

So if you want a good, stiff test of your capacity to love, go into your favorite store some day – preferably when there is a sale – and see if you can walk straight through, looking neither left nor right, and come out unscathed. It may sound unbelievable, but it *can* be done.

*I have learned through bitter experience the
one supreme lesson to conserve my anger,
and as heat conserved is transmuted into
energy, even so our anger controlled can
be transmuted into a power that can
move the world.*

MAHATMA GANDHI

Mahatma Gandhi provides a perfect example of
how anger can be harnessed. As a young, unknown, brown-skinned lawyer traveling in
South Africa on business, he was roughly
thrown from the train because he refused to surrender his first-class ticket and move to the
third-class compartment. He spent a cold,
sleepless night on the railway platform.

Later, he said this was the turning point of his
life: for on that night, full of anger because of this
personal injustice, as well as the countless injustices suffered by so many others every day in
South Africa, he resolved not to rest until he had
set those injustices right. On that night he con-
quered his anger and vowed to resist injustice,
not by violence or retaliation, but through the
loving power of nonviolent resistance, which
elevates the consciousness of both oppressed
and oppressor.

We may never be called on to liberate a
people, or lead a vast nation, but Gandhi's example can apply in a small way in our own lives,
when we decide to return goodwill for ill will,
love for hatred, in the innumerable little acts of
daily life.

I look upon all creatures equally; none are
less dear to me and none more dear. But
those who worship me with love live in me,
and I come to life in them.

SRI KRISHNA (BHAGAVAD GITA)

There is no need to compare ourselves with others, or to feel our contribution is less important than someone else's. Yesterday I read a story that makes this point very well. It was about a Hasidic rabbi named Susya, who said, "When I die, I will not be asked, 'Why weren't you more like Moses?' I will be asked, 'Why weren't you more like Susya?'"

Similarly, Sri Krishna is not going to say, "You could have been a doctor! Why were you just a nurse's aide?" He is going to ask, "Were you the best nurse's aide you knew how to be? Did you help your patients not just by your labor, but by your genuine concern for their welfare?" Each of us has a special gift, some special capacity by which we can contribute to the welfare of those around us. What is important is that we use that gift or skill to the very best of our ability.

In tribulation, immediately draw near to
God with confidence, and you will receive
strength, enlightenment, and instruction.

SAINT JOHN OF THE CROSS

I confess that I have always been sensitive to pain. When I was a little boy, I hurt my leg playing soccer. It became infected, so my granny took me to our doctor. He washed the wound as gently as he could while I winced. Then he told me apologetically, "I'm going to have to apply tincture of iodine."

Now, I had heard many stories about how much it hurt to have iodine applied to a wound. So I closed my eyes. I felt the doctor's touch on my leg, and then a wave of pain across the wound. I think my yell must have lifted the roof.

Then I noticed the pain had subsided, so I opened my eyes. "Is it over?" I asked. The doctor looked at me with compassion and said, "I haven't even applied the iodine yet."

Often it is fear of pain, and the resistance to pain, that makes pain hard to bear. When fear goes, suffering becomes manageable; and the mantram is the best thing I know for banishing fear. Whether it is a headache, a stomachache, or serious injury, the mantram always helps.

*Those who are more adapted to the active
life can prepare themselves for contemplation
in the practice of the active life, while those
who are more adapted to the contemplative
life can take upon themselves the works
of the active life so as to become yet
more apt for contemplation.*

SAINT THOMAS AQUINAS

There are a number of very practical steps you can take to make your meditation better. One, be sure you have enough selfless work to harness the energy released in meditation, to channel it toward the welfare of all. A deeper level of consciousness brings more resources, more energy; if these are not utilized selflessly, they are going to cause trouble. The deeper your meditation, the harder you need to work.

In fact, one of the simplest ways to assess your meditation is to look at your performance at work. How punctual are you? How concentrated? How harmoniously can you cooperate with your co-workers? Can you work with complete concentration, yet drop your work at will when the time comes to drop it? The answers to questions like these reveal a lot about interior progress.

*Old age is the most unexpected of all the
things that can happen to a man.*

LEON TROTSKY

When the first grey hair appears on our head, it is a critical juncture in life. We go to the mirror with a sinking feeling of dread and try to pluck out the evidence – one here, two there. But the more we pull out, the more seem to come in.

I tease my friends by asking which of them would like to relive their adolescence. It always brings a groan. Youth has a lot to offer, but so does the experience of age. In India we have a joke about a man going to a barber and asking, "Do you have anything for grey hair?" "Yes," the barber says, "respect." Just because we don't have wrinkles or a grey hair, we are not necessarily alive in the fullest sense of the word. Real living comes from making a contribution to life.

This is the paradox of life: when we cling to the body, it loses its beauty. But when we do not cling to the body – and use it as an instrument given us to serve others – it glows with a special beauty, as we can see from the lives of many great mystics. When our consciousness becomes pure, even the body begins to reflect its light.

Lord, make me an instrument of thy peace.
Where there is hatred, let me sow love.
SAINT FRANCIS OF ASSISI

When we ask to be made instruments of peace, what we are really asking for is the boundless determination to empty ourselves of every state of mind that disrupts relationships – anger, resentment, jealousy, greed, self-will in any form. Our first priority is to reform ourselves; without that, how can we expect to help other people reform themselves? It is the living example of a man or woman giving all they have to making love a reality that moves our hearts to follow. We do not need a bumper sticker that says, "You are following an instrument of the Lord." Our everyday actions speak for themselves.

Still your mind in Me, still yourself in Me,
and without doubt you shall be united with
Me, Lord of Love dwelling in your heart.

SRI KRISHNA (BHAGAVAD GITA)

Children attending their first swimming lessons have a healthy fear of putting their faces under water. They are afraid they are going to drown. This is the feeling we can get when we go deeper in meditation and begin to break loose from some of our long-cherished emotional attachments. When I was first meditating, I had the same fears everyone has. All kinds of struggles were going on inside me, and it took time and effort to overcome them. But once the waters closed over my head and I began to get my bearings in these new realms, I knew this was what I had been looking for and longing for, and all my energy went into diving deeper.

When we put our heads under and dive deep, leaving selfishness on the surface, we find a joy that is a million times what any surface sensation can give, and a love that at its fullest expression embraces all of life. Initially we may fear losing the sensory satisfactions that lie on the surface, but waiting far below are infinite joy, infinite love, infinite life.

Thou art my glory, and the exultation
of my heart, Thou art my hope and refuge
in the time of my trouble.

THOMAS A KEMPIS

Devotion to a personal God has enabled many of the world's greatest mystics to cross the bridge from fragmented consciousness to unified, total consciousness.

When we have traveled a certain way into our consciousness through sustained, untiring, unflagging effort, we eventually come to a point where our progress is stopped cold. There before us is a yawning chasm, waiting to swallow us up. In such cases we are not going to make it to the other side by plodding along one step at a time, which is our usual humble pace.

We will have to make a tremendous leap. Complete devotion to the Lord as personified in a divine incarnation will enable us to soar. At that time, we will close our eyes and say, "I do not have the capacity to go farther without your help, Lord. Now it is up to you." We'll jump into the fathomless darkness – secure in the faith that he will never let us fall but will carry us safely in his arms to the other side.

*Like a ball batted back and forth, a human
being is batted by two forces within.*

YOGABINDU UPANISHAD

As human beings we have a divided nature –
partly physical, but essentially spiritual. We are
constantly batted by two conflicting forces.
One force is the fierce downward thrust of our
past conditioning as separate, self-oriented,
physical creatures. Yet, built into our very nature is an inner drive that will not let us be
satisfied with a life governed only by biological
laws. Some inner evolutionary imperative is
constantly exhorting us to grow, to reach for the
highest that we can conceive.

How sweet it is to love, and to be dissolved,
and as it were to bathe myself in thy love.

THOMAS A KEMPIS

In these times, a common prescription for a day
packed with troubles is to go jump in your hot
tub. Relaxation starts immediately; for a time, at
least, the body is at peace.

Now imagine a hot tub for the mind. That is
what meditation is; it can bathe your mind in re-
laxing thoughts. This requires a lot of practice,
but when you have learned to jump in the hot tub
of meditation at the end of a day, instead of re-
hashing problems with your co-workers or
downing a double martini, you can close your
eyes, start in with an inspirational passage, and
let the accumulated tensions of the day dissolve.

*Of all things that are, nothing is forbidden
and nothing is contrary to God but one thing
only: that is, self-will, or to will otherwise
than as the Eternal Will would have it. . . .
And could a man, while on earth, be wholly
quit of self-will and ownership, and stand up
free and at large in God's true light, and
continue therein, he would be sure of
the Kingdom of Heaven.*

THEOLOGIA GERMANICA

All spiritual progress requires the sacrifice of
self-will. Since most of us have rather large
amounts of self-will, we cannot expect to get rid
of it overnight. Those who are terribly eager
may expect to load all their selfishness in one big
truck and in one grand gesture cart it all to the
dump. Unfortunately, there is no truck big
enough, and even if there were, we would not
have the strength to get all our self-will into it.

The safest and simplest method is to cart off a
little bit of selfishness every day, day after day,
year after year. A thousand and one little acts of
thoughtfulness displace a monstrous load. One
day we find to our great surprise that all our separateness has vacated the premises. Then we will
see that the "sacrifice" was no sacrifice at all. We
have lost nothing, but have gained everything.

*Now you may ask, How can we come to
perceive this direct leading of God? By a
careful looking at home, and abiding within
the gates of thy own soul. Therefore, let a
man be at home in his own heart, and cease
from his restless chase of and search
after outward things.*

JOHANNES TAULER

Whatever you are enmeshed in personally during the day is likely to follow you into your
meditation. Part of your attention will be on
that. It will act like an inflatable inner tube
around your middle, preventing you from diving below the surface. No attachment is worth
the price you will pay. You can take my word for
it, and the word of the world's great saints and
mystics, too. I assure you that in letting go of
selfish attachments, you are not losing anything
except your frustration; you are not letting go of
anything but your old insecurities.

While you are meditating, concentrate completely on the inspirational passage. When your
concentration is complete, you will not have any
impediments; you will sink naturally deeper and
deeper. Then, no distraction will have any compelling force behind it. It will not bother you; it
will not oppress you; it will have no power to
deflect you from your purpose.

But they for whom I am the supreme goal,
who do all work renouncing self for me
and meditate on me with single-hearted
devotion, these I will swiftly rescue from
death's vast sea, for their consciousness
has entered into me.

SRI KRISHNA (BHAGAVAD GITA)

When the lover of God finds somebody in danger, he doesn't turn away. He runs to help. This is one of the unmistakable signs of true love of God.

When someone is in trouble, you don't say, "How did he behave towards me?" You don't ask, "Of what race or color is she?" or "Is this person my countryman? Does she belong to my religion?" None of these questions can be asked by the person who truly loves God. He or she just runs to the rescue of the person in trouble.

When we are trying to help someone, it is *we* who get great joy out of it. If we try to rescue someone who has been unkind, the joy is even greater. This is a secret all but forgotten in our modern world: we find a much more lasting joy in rescuing others than in trying to save ourselves, because in rescuing others we are making sure that we will be saved by the Lord who is within.

Wherever you go, you will always bear
yourself about with you, and so you
will always find yourself.

THOMAS A KEMPIS

There is only one way to get a real vacation: get as far away from the ego as possible. Worrying about your problems all the time makes for misery with a capital *M*. For getting away from misery, I recommend this "economy plan": do not feed your ego and your problems, with your attention. They will slowly lose weight.

When we feed them, constantly begging them to have one more helping even when they are gorged, we acquire obese problems that hug us tightly and weight us down. So if you really want a vacation, do not brood on your troubles. Do not let yourself get jealous or say uncharitable things about anyone. In other words, do not give the ego breakfast in bed; do not pack it a bag lunch; do not fix its dinner; do not give it pocket money for buying snacks; do not even give it a glass of water. Slowly, surely, the ego will lose weight, until one fine day it will be nothing but a thin ghost of its former self. You will be able to see right through it, to the divine presence that shines in each of us.

Love seeketh not itself to please,
Nor for itself hath any care,
But for another gives its ease,
And builds a Heaven in Hell's despair.

WILLIAM BLAKE

Though I have lived in this country for many years now, there are still many American expressions that I don't understand. I remember trying to explain meditation to a young fellow in Berkeley who kept shaking his head and saying, "Man, I just don't hear you." In all innocence, I started over again a little louder. Finally it dawned on me what he really meant: "I just don't *want* to hear you. I don't like what you're saying."

This is what most of us do when there is disagreement. We carry around a pair of earplugs, and the minute somebody starts saying something we don't like, we stuff them in our ears until he or she is through. Watch with some detachment the next time you find yourself quarreling with someone you love. It won't look like a melodrama, but like a first-rate comedy – two people trying to reach an understanding by not listening to each other!

An effective way of dealing with a disagreement is simply to listen with complete attention, even if we don't care for what the other person is saying. We are showing how our respect won't waver no matter how vehemently we may disagree.

*The words of the tongue
should have three gatekeepers.*

ARAB PROVERB

Before words get past the lips, the first gate-keeper asks, "Is this true?" That stops a lot of traffic immediately. But if the words get past the first gatekeeper, there is a second who asks, "Is it kind?" And for those words that qualify here too, the last gatekeeper asks: "Is it necessary?"

With these three on guard, most of us would find very little to say. Here I think it is necessary to make exceptions in the interests of good company and let the third gatekeeper look the other way now and then. After all, a certain amount of pleasant conversation is part of the artistry of living. But the first two gatekeepers should always be on duty.

It is so easy to say something at the expense of another for the purpose of enhancing our own image. But such remarks – irresistible as they may be – serve only to fatten our own egos and agitate others. We should be so fearful of hurting people that even if a clever remark is rushing off our tongue, we can barricade the gate. We should be able to swallow our cleverness rather than hurt someone. Better to say something banal but harmless than to be clever at someone else's expense.

*In the first days of my youth I tried to find it
in the creatures, as I saw others do; but the
more I sought, the less I found it, and the
nearer I went to it, the further off it was. For
of every image that appeared to me, before I
had fully tested it, or abandoned myself to
peace in it, an inner voice said to me:
"This is not what thou seekest."*

HEINRICH SUSO

Physical attraction is not a firm foundation on
which to build a relationship, for the simple reason that it is never constant. It sets in motion a
cycle of expectation and disillusionment that
can go on and on. The person who lives in a
world of fantasy will often blame the other for
letting him down. Perhaps, for example, Juliet
expects Romeo to come to her balcony every
morning and launch into, "It is the east, and you
are the sun. . . ." Three days after the honeymoon, she feels crushed when she is greeted at
breakfast with nothing more romantic than,
"Where's the toast?" Many relationships sput-
ter because of just such inflated expectations,
which demand of life something that it simply
cannot give.

We should not feel that close relationships are
infeasible, but they *are* demanding. Through
experience, we come to realize that in love nothing comes as easily as we expected. Everything
beautiful has to be worked for.

Where there is injury, let me sow pardon.

SAINT FRANCIS OF ASSISI

Once, in wintertime, it is said that Francis and his disciple Brother Leo were making a hard journey on foot through the snowy countryside of Italy. They had been walking along in silence for a long time when Brother Leo turned to Francis and asked him, "How can we find perfect joy?" Francis stopped and replied, "Even if all our friars were perfect in their holiness and could work all kinds of miracles for others, we still would not have perfect joy."

He turned and walked on, and Brother Leo ran after him. "Then what is perfect joy?" Francis stopped again, "Even if we could speak with the birds of the air and the beasts of the field and know all the secrets of nature, we still would not have perfect joy. Even if we could cure all the ills on the face of the earth, we would still not have found perfect joy."

Brother Leo was practically shouting: "Then please, Father Francis, what *is* the secret of perfect joy?"

"Brother, suppose we go to that monastery across the field and tell the gatekeeper how weary and cold we are, and he calls us tramps and beats us and throws us out into the winter night. Then, Brother, if we can say with love in our hearts, 'Bless you in the name of Jesus,' then we shall have found perfect joy."

People do not know what the Name of God
can do. Those who repeat it constantly alone
know its power. It can purify our mind
completely. . . . The Name can take us to the
summit of spiritual experience.

SWAMI RAMDAS

The desire of our soul is to thy name,
and to the remembrance of thee.

ISAIAH

A friend who is a doctor tells me that no one
really knows how aspirin works. Yet we have
faith in aspirin. When you take the bottle off the
bathroom shelf and pop a couple of pills into
your mouth, you are saying in effect, "I believe.
I have faith that this will work."

I would say, "Take plenty of mantrams too."
It is equally good advice: one relieves fever in the
body, the other, the fever of self-will. People
sometimes scoff at this and retort, "We don't
think it will work." I reply, "Don't you think
you can give the Buddha or Jesus as much cre-
dence as you give Mr. Bayer?"

Try it. If you only feel comforted by things
that come in a bottle, take an empty bottle and
write *Rama, Rama* or *Jesus, Jesus* on the label.
Then put it on your bathroom shelf. When you
have a disquieting afternoon or evening or night,
take it down, look at it, and start repeating
Rama, Rama or *Jesus, Jesus.* You have taken the
medicine.

*He who would be serene and pure needs
but one thing, detachment.*

MEISTER ECKHART

Most of us identify ourselves with our pet opinions. Then, when we are contradicted, we take it personally and get upset. If we could look at ourselves with some detachment, we would see how absurd this is. There is scarcely any more connection between me and my opinions than there is between me and my car. I have a close friend who is devoted to her Volkswagen "bug." If I compliment her on it, she is pleased; if I tell her what Ralph Nader says about Volkswagens, she feels insulted. But why? Where is the connection? *She* is not a VW "bug."

Once we realize at a deeper level of consciousness that we are not our opinions, most of the resentment in differences of opinion disappears. There is nothing wrong with disagreement. In fact, sometimes it is necessary to disagree. But we should do so with complete respect for the other person.

Where are you searching for me, friend?
Look! Here am I right within you.
Not in temple, nor in mosque,
Not in Kaaba, nor Kailas,
But here right within you am I.

KABIR

Some of the most magnificent figures in the history of mysticism have begun the spiritual search while still suffering from severe personal problems. Saint Augustine was deeply enmeshed in the life of the world, and pulled himself free only after great anguish of mind. Others suffered physically. Saint Therese of Lisieux endured the constant pain of tuberculosis. So there is no need for any of us to feel downcast about our situation or the particular difficulties we face, provided we do everything we can to purify our mind.

Meditation is essentially a discipline for slowing down the furious pace of thinking; if you can gradually bring your mind to a state so still that no movement, no thought, can arise except those you yourself approve, your mind will have become pure. We have no need to teach pure motives to the mind. All that is necessary to make the mind pure is to undo the negative conditioning to which it has been subjected; then we will be left with pure, unconditioned awareness.

Though God be everywhere present, yet He is only present in thee in the deepest and most central part of thy soul. . . . This depth is called the centre, the fund or bottom of the soul. . . . Awake, then, thou that sleepest, and Christ, who from all eternity has been espoused to thy soul, shall give thee light. Begin to search and dig in thine own field for this pearl of eternity that lies hidden in it; it cannot cost thee too much, nor canst thou buy it too dear, for it is all; and when thou hast found it thou wilt know that all which thou hast sold or given away for it is as mere a nothing as a bubble upon the water.

WILLIAM LAW

Living on the surface of life as we do, we don't suspect what a treasure trove of love and wisdom we have within. If I knew of a simple, painless way of unlocking this treasure, I would be the first to give it. But as far as I know, there is no way to enter and make use of these untold riches except by practicing meditation and integrating its allied disciplines into our daily life. There is no shortcut around the travail of this journey into consciousness, and those who have traversed it testify that it is the ultimate test of human endurance.

Yet it is the very challenge that appeals to people. It banishes boredom and brings the dew of freshness to every day.

*Now the Name of Jesus is a concrete
and powerful means of transfiguring men
and women into their hidden,
innermost, utmost reality.*

ON THE INVOCATION OF THE
NAME OF JESUS

If we could interview a negative tendency, say, Resentment, it might say, "I don't worry! I've been safely in this fellow's mind for years. He takes good care of me – feeds me, dwells on me, brings me out and parades me around! All I have to do is roar and stir things up from time to time. Yes, I'm getting fat and feeling grand. And I'm proud to tell you there are even a few little rancors and vituperations running around now, spawned by yours truly!"

So he may think. But when you repeat the mantram, you are prying him loose. You are saying, in a way that goes beyond vows and good intentions, that resentment is no part of the real you. You no longer acknowledge its right to exist.

We use something genuine to drive out impostors that have roamed about largely through our neglect and helplessness. We move closer and closer to our divine Self, because these impostors, resentment and ill will, are no longer coming between us.

*I went to the root of things,
and found nothing but Him alone.*

MIRA BAI

The Lord is not someone outside us, who lived in a given place at a given time. He is right within. Throughout creation, God is the principle of creativity itself.

Even some of the greatest scientists and philosophers have yet to grasp this simple truth. One well-respected astronomer calls it cowardly to conclude that God created the universe just because we cannot comprehend the conditions of its creation. This great scientist is still thinking of God as someone outside, holding court beyond the Andromeda galaxy; he hasn't glimpsed that all this *is* God, and wherever there is light, or beauty, or excellence in anything, we are seeing a little more of His glory.

But, as Mira says, to see this vision we cannot just stay on the surface of life picking up a few baubles of pleasure and prestige. We have to get deep, deep below, and go to the root of all things.

Acquire a firm will and the utmost patience.

ANANDAMAYI MA

We begin our journey towards the supreme goal of life from where we stand. Just as it is good to be patient with others, it is equally necessary to be patient with ourselves. After all, when the desire to lead the spiritual life and live for others comes to us, we can be haunted by our past mistakes, by the amount of time we have wasted in selfish pursuits. But we must accept ourselves with all our strengths and weaknesses.

There are many obstacles on the spiritual path which can strengthen us, and these cannot be overcome unless we have infinite patience with ourselves. If we are patient with others, shouldn't we be patient with ourselves as well? Each of us is individual, with our own special qualities. We start now, where we are, with our partial love for money, partial love for pleasure, partial love for prestige, and a little love for the Lord. All of us, no matter what our past has been, no matter what our present drawbacks are, can take to the spiritual life, and we will progress at our own pace. It is not good to compare one person's progress with another's.

*Tell me, where is the soul's abode? – Upon
the pinions of the wind.*

MEISTER ECKHART

*We ought to fly away from earth to heaven
as quickly as we can; and to fly away is to
become like God, as far as this is possible;
and to become like him, is to become
holy, just, and wise.*

PLATO

We are all capable of flying like eagles high in the sky of love. But often we prefer running on the ground instead.

Have you seen that curious bird, the quail? We have many of them where we live. When we are driving down the lane, they won't get out of the way. They won't fly. They try to outrun the car. It is only when they conclude their number is up that they start flying. They know how to fly, but they would rather stay on the ground.

Most of us are like that. But mystics like Eckhart tell us that our wings are there, we have only to spread them to experience the exhilaration of soaring into the sky and looking down to see all life as one.

The Perfect Way is only difficult for those
who pick and choose;
Do not like, do not dislike;
all will then be clear.
Make a hairbreadth difference,
and Heaven and Earth are set apart.

SENG-TS'AN

Happiness and sorrow, good and bad, pleasure and pain – these are the very texture of life on the superficial level. Self-will thrives on these dualities, responding with infinite likes and dislikes, which are the ego's way of self-expression. The less you are bound by likes and dislikes, the more clearly you will be able to see the core of purity and selflessness that is the real Self in everyone, even in people who cause trouble.

My grandmother had a pungent phrase for difficult people: "A lash in the eye." We all know from experience how an eyelash in the eye can be so irritating that we just cannot think about anything else. That is exactly how difficult people affect those around them. So most of us try to avoid such people.

But for the mystics, this lash in the eye is an opportunity for learning the skills that matter most in life: patience, forgiveness, and freedom from likes and dislikes. They go and put their arm around someone who has given them a really difficult time, and say sincerely, "Without you, how could I ever have learned to be patient? How could I have learned to forgive?"

*Endurance is one of the most difficult
disciplines, but it is to the one who endures
that the final victory comes.*

THE BUDDHA

People often find that meditation is easy for the
first few months; but then, just when they think
things are going well, it becomes difficult. It is
like digging in your garden. The surface level of
consciousness is soft loam, easy digging for the
first twelve inches or so. The blade of the shovel
is turning over the soil so easily that you say,
"This is great! Isn't meditation wonderful?"
Then you strike something hard and impenetrable. Your hands sting from the shock, and your
arms ache. That is the first stratum of bedrock –
a dense, rock-hard layer of sheer resistance.
Congratulations! You are getting somewhere at
last!

How do you know you have hit something?
The most common sign is a wave of sleep during
meditation. Your mind is saying, in effect, "My
shovel is getting blunted, and my arms are tired.
Why not stop digging and have a snooze?" It is
extremely important not to yield to this inclination. Sit up straighter and draw away from your
back support until the wave of sleep has passed.
This problem of sleep may be with you for a long
time. You have a lot of strata to dig through. But
there is great joy in this digging.

*Take God for your spouse and friend and
walk with Him continually, and you will not
sin and will learn to love, and the things you
must do will work out prosperously for you.*

SAINT JOHN OF THE CROSS

A tremendous amount of vital energy is consumed in thinking about sense pleasures. Think of how high your electric bill would be at the end of the month if you left your lights on all the time. Houses have switches, so we can turn off the lights when we don't need them. We often forget that we have switches, too, so we can turn off inappropriate desires. When the mind is clamoring for something, say for a fattening midnight snack, repeat the mantram. For a while there will be a struggle. The mind will say *Rama, Rama,* then a little voice will chime in, "Surely there's no harm in a little cookie? Or maybe just a helping of frozen yogurt?" Don't pay any attention to the little voice, but keep repeating the mantram. After a while, with practice, the mind will settle back down to tranquillity.

There is great satisfaction in being able to let a desire arise at the proper time and to keep it still at other times. We lose nothing in this. The man or woman who gains some mastery over the thinking process finds that the senses have become faithful servants. This is not bleaching the color out of life; it is gaining mastery over our desire so that we can conserve all our vital energy and put it to use wisely and selflessly.

*If someone takes your coat, give him your
cloak as well; if he makes you go a mile
with him, go with him two.*

THE GOSPEL ACCORDING TO
SAINT MATTHEW

If you really want to land a blow at a compulsion, defy it. Do just the opposite of what it says. It is a daring approach which appeals to everyone with a sense of adventure. If somebody has been unkind to you, go out of your way to be kind to him. It can require a lot of endurance simply to be patient with such a person, but we're talking about more than endurance now; we're talking about daring.

Try it: there is an exhilaration in it, and a special delight in seeing the other person rub his eyes in disbelief, "I was just rude to that chap, and now he's being thoughtful. What's wrong with him?"

For where there is true love, a man is neither
out of measure lifted up by prosperity, nor
cast down by mishap; whether you give or
take away from him, so long as he keeps his
beloved, he has a spring of inward peace.
Thus, even though thy outward man grieve,
or weep downright, that may well be borne,
if only thy inner man remain at peace,
perfectly content with the will of God.

JOHANNES TAULER

Try putting the welfare of those around you first, especially when you are feeling discouraged or depressed. I would like to rewrite the old song to say, "Oh, what a beautiful morning! Oh, what a beautiful day! Everything's going *your* way."

Some doctors are telling us now that this kind of attitude may be a shield against illness. A recent article went so far as to say, "Amiability – plain old good-naturedness – seems to have a protective effect on health." In the same article, one of the recommended cures for chronic hostility was, "Try to be more forgiving." This is advice as old as the hills.

Most of us do not understand that when we live in a world of ill will, as millions of people do, nursing grievances so anger can't die a natural death, we are creating an internal environment that surrounds us with a poison worse than smog twenty-four hours a day. When we reduce our hostility, we're cleaning up the inner air, and we will find unsuspected benefits not only for the mind, but for the body as well.

The soul that is attached to anything,
however much good there may be in it, will
not arrive at the liberty of divine union. For
whether it be a strong wire rope or a slender
and delicate thread that holds the bird, it
matters not, if it really holds it fast; for, until
the cord be broken, the bird cannot fly.

SAINT JOHN OF THE CROSS

As long as we are caught in selfish attachments, we will not be able to live in awareness of the divine unity of all life. Remember Jonathan Swift's description of Gulliver tied with thousands of little strings anchored to the ground with thousands of little pegs? Similarly, we are tied down to our sorrow and suffering by numerous selfish attachments, large and small.

We can get attached to anything, from our heirloom china to our comic books. Things are not meant to be loved but to be used wisely. People are to be loved, but there, too, we must be careful not to come to see people as possessions – which is quite different from loving them. Through the practice of meditation, we can learn to recall all our selfish desires and slip free of the fetters that bind us to a limited way of life. For it is then, when you are not selfishly attached to anything, when you are living for the welfare of everybody around you, that you are likely to be given a long life, health, and plenty of energy to go on contributing to the peace of the world in whatever way you can.

Go seek, O mind, go seek
Vrindavan in your heart,
Where with his loving devotees
Sri Krishna sports eternally.

BENGALI HYMN

Vrindavan is the sylvan setting of Sri Krishna's boyhood, where the Lord and his playmates were always dancing, full of joy. The real Vrindavan, the kingdom of heaven, is within; when you enter it, you will live in that joy continuously.

Radha, the lovely village girl of Vrindavan, represents the human heart longing for the Lord. Radha is head over heels in love with Krishna, and she waits for a tryst with him, sure he *must* come to her someday. She puts on her most alluring makeup, braids her hair with jasmine, puts on her best silk sari and jewelry, and then she waits . . . and waits.

"I hear him coming!" But it's only the leaves of the trees rustling in the wind. "I hear his flute!" But it's just the nightingale. And the longer she waits, the more her passions fuse. Finally, all her longing is transmuted into all-consuming love of Krishna. That is the reason the Lord puts us through this loving agony. He simply waits until we are ready, for until then he cannot come.

Beauty is all very well at first sight;
but who ever looks at it when it has
been in the house three days?

GEORGE BERNARD SHAW

Often we try to build relationships on what is pleasing to us, particularly on physical attraction. But if there is anything sure about physical attraction, it is that it *has* to change. We cannot build on it; its very nature is to come and go.

Physical attraction is a sensation – here one minute and gone the next. Love is a relationship. It *is* pleasant to be with someone who is physically attractive, but how long can you enjoy an aquiline nose? How long can you thrill to the timbre of a voice when it doesn't say what you like? It's very much like eating: no matter how much you are attracted to chocolate pie, there is a limit to how much of it you can enjoy. Beyond that limit, if somebody merely mentions chocolate, your stomach stages a revolt.

If you want to build a relationship, build it on what endures. To build on a firm foundation, we have to stop asking, "What do I like?" and ask only, "What can I give?" Then there is joy in everything, because there is joy in the relationship itself – in ups *and* downs, through the pleasant and the unpleasant, in sickness and in health.

*Late have I loved thee, O Beauty so ancient
and so new; late have I loved thee! For
behold, thou wert within me and I outside;
and I sought thee outside and in my
unloveliness fell upon these lovely things that
thou hast made. Thou wert with me and I
was not with thee. I was kept from thee by
those things, yet had they not been in thee,
they would not have been at all. Thou didst
call and cry to me and break open my
deafness; and thou didst send forth thy
beams and shine upon me and chase away
my blindness; thou didst breathe fragrance
upon me, and I drew in my breath and do
now pant for thee. I tasted thee, and now
hunger and thirst for thee; thou didst touch
me, and now I burn for thy peace.*

SAINT AUGUSTINE

When mystics use the word *love*, they use it
very carefully, in the deeply spiritual sense,
where to love is to know; to love is to act.

If you really love, from the depths of your
consciousness, that love gives you a native wisdom. You perceive the needs of others intuitively and clearly, with detachment from any
personal desires; and you know how to act creatively to meet those needs, dexterously sur-
mounting any obstacle that comes in the way.
Such is the immense, driving power of love.

*There is nothing so disobedient as an
undisciplined mind, and there is nothing
so obedient as a disciplined mind.*

THE BUDDHA

Attention is very much like a dog. Recently my
friend Steve acquired a large, affectionate, and
utterly blithe-spirited retriever pup whom his
son has named Ganesha. Ganesha has a lot of energy, and he has never been trained; he is accus-
tomed to doing whatever he likes. If you put
him in the yard, he digs under the fence. Leave
him in the bedroom and he chews up your slip-
pers. Take him for a walk and the next thing you
know, he is halfway across a field chasing a deer.

So Steve has started to train him. For a while,
I thought it was the other way around: Ganesha
would bark and then Steve would run after him.
But now, after a lot of patient training, Ganesha
has learned to heel and to stay.

Attention can be trained in a similar way
through the practice of meditation and one-
pointedness. At first it wanders restlessly all
over, looking into everything and everybody.
But through training, it becomes an alert, con-
genial companion.

*The test of a man or woman's breeding
is how they behave in a quarrel.*

GEORGE BERNARD SHAW

When tempers are frayed, and an argument is in progress, it is very difficult for anyone to listen with courtesy to an opposing point of view. If we could ask the mind on such occasions why it doesn't listen, it would answer candidly, "Why should I? I already know I'm right." We may not put it into words, but the other person gets the message: "You're not worth listening to." It is this lack of respect that offends people in an argument, much more than any difference of opinion.

But respect can be learned – in part by acting as if we had respect. We show respect by simply listening with complete attention. Try it and see: the action is very much like that of a classical drama. For a while there is "rising action." The other person's temper keeps going up; language becomes more and more vivid; everything is heading for a climax. But then comes the denouement. The other person begins to quiet down: his voice becomes gentler, his language kinder, all because you have not retaliated or lost your respect for him.

O good Jesu Thou has bound my heart in the
thought of Thy Name, and now I can not but
sing it; therefore have mercy upon me,
making perfect that Thou hast ordained.

RICHARD ROLLE

When you are walking is one of the best times
to repeat the mantram, especially if you walk
briskly. The rhythm of your footsteps, the
rhythm of the mantram, and the rhythm of your
breathing all harmonize to soothe and invigo-
rate the body and mind. Breathing is closely
connected with our state of mind. People who
are tense or angry breathe rapidly and irregu-
larly; those who are calm, loving, and secure
breathe like a little child, smoothly, slowly, and
deeply. A brisk walk helps to make your breathing rhythm deep and even, and the mantram will
help to calm your mind.

*By two wings a man is lifted up from
things earthly: by simplicity and purity.*

THOMAS A KEMPIS

To soar to the heights, the soul needs two wings. One is purity, which enables us to keep our eyes on the one thing in life that matters: awareness of the divinity within every human being. The other is simplicity: of life-style, but also simplicity in our desires, so that we can gradually withdraw our love and loyalty from every pursuit that does not nurture awareness of God.

This raises a worry that many serious-minded people have today. Living in the workaday world, surrounded by all manner of influences we cannot control, can purity and simplicity ever be anything for us but beautiful abstractions? It is one thing to grasp intellectually how we want to live. It is quite another to put our ideals into practice.

Yet, we will find that as our commitment to a more spiritual life deepens, we learn to tug our attention away from lesser things, and focus on what really matters. And, to our great surprise, we will actually hit on some remedies. One person may start with his teenaged son, discovering a way to give him support that hadn't occurred to him before. Another may mobilize help for children dying of hunger in Ethiopia, or help the homeless in the inner city.

*If you let your mind dwell on ghosts, you'll
become a ghost yourself. If you fix your mind
on God your life will be filled with God.
Now – which are you going to choose?*

SRI RAMAKRISHNA

In meditation, we learn the skill of bringing our
attention back to the words of the inspirational
passage whenever it strays away. Attention is
like a restless puppy, fond of running after anything new that comes along. When it sees an in-
tensely charged memory, it cannot let it roll by;
it has to chase the memory and keep yapping,
yapping, yapping.

Just as with a dog, we have to call the mind
back over and over again, whenever we sit down
for meditation. This may go on for years. But if
we keep practicing diligently and systematically, the day will come when we can put our attention where we want it with little effort, and it
will stay without movement or protest. Then,
however unkind somebody may have been, we
will not be mastered by resentment; our attention will not turn to the past at all.

Great is this power of memory, exceedingly great, O my God, a spreading and limitless room within me. Who can reach its uttermost depth? Here are men going afar to marvel at the heights of mountains, the mighty waves of the sea, the long courses of great rivers, the vastness of the ocean, the movements of the stars, yet they leave themselves unnoticed!

SAINT AUGUSTINE

Today many people who enjoy traveling are not content with visiting London or Paris; they want to travel by camel in the Sahara, or kayak in the Antarctic. But no matter how exotic, this is horizontal travel, where we stay on the surface of life. Much more fascinating is vertical travel – that is, meditation, which takes us to the Land of Love in the utmost depths of consciousness.

For a long time we may not get very far, but if we insist on traveling deep, meditation will become a daring adventure. We will pass through level after level of consciousness, just the way one travels from one country to another. There is this difference: when we pass from the United States into Mexico, we know when we have crossed the border. We must stop and speak to the guard. Then the language changes. We know we are in a new land. In meditation, it is rather different. The changes are likely to take place so gradually that we may not even be aware of it immediately. But slowly and surely we will begin to have a strong feeling of coming home to our native land.

It is in pardoning that we are pardoned.
SAINT FRANCIS OF ASSISI

There are times when past mistakes swim into our vision and do their best to consume us in guilt or regret. At such times it is essential to repeat the mantram and turn all our attention outwards, away from ourselves. Analyzing our mistakes and dwelling on how to repay them is of no earthly benefit at all. If, when you were in Milwaukee, you happened to say something insulting about your girlfriend's dog, it is not necessary to go to Milwaukee and find your old girlfriend or her dog to make amends. Every dog you treat with kindness will be a proxy for that dog. If you have treated a particular person badly, even if you can no longer win that person's forgiveness, you can still win the forgiveness of yourself, of the Lord of Love within, by bearing with people who treat you badly and doing your best not to treat anyone badly again. Whatever we have done, we can always make amends for it without ever looking back in guilt or sorrow.

And what rule do you think I walked by?
Truly a strange one, but the best in the whole
world. I was guided by an implicit faith in
God's goodness; and therefore led to the
study of the most obvious and common
things. For thus I thought within myself:
God being, as generally believed , infinite in
goodness, it is most consonant and agreeable
with His nature that the best things
should be most common.

THOMAS TRAHERNE

A state of permanent joy, hidden at the very center of consciousness, is the Eden to which the long journey of spiritual seeking leads. There, the mystics of all religions agree, we uncover our original goodness. We don't have to buy it; we don't have to create it; we don't have to pour it in; we don't even have to be worthy of it. This native goodness is the essential core of human nature.

We are made, the scriptures of all religions assure us, in the image of God. Nothing can change our original goodness. Whatever mistakes we have made in the past, whatever problems we may have in the present, in every one of us the uncreated spark in the soul remains untouched, ever pure, ever perfect. Even if we try with all our might to douse or hide it, it is always ready to set our personality ablaze with light.

When the heart grieves over what it has lost,
the spirit rejoices over what it has found.

SUFI EPIGRAM

During the early stages of the spiritual journey, we can feel a certain deprivation when we have to keep saying no to the senses as they clamor for things that will only add to the burden of the journey later on. "Don't eat this. Don't drink that. Don't smoke this. Don't watch that." This is what you hear from your spiritual teacher. There is no rapture; there is no ecstasy; only "keep plugging along."

This discriminating restraint of the senses is not asceticism. Its purpose is not to subjugate the body. We need to train the senses to be faithful allies on our journey for two compelling reasons: first, the body is our vehicle, and we need to keep it healthy, strong, and resilient so that it can carry us steadily and safely to the summit of consciousness; second, training the senses strengthens the will day by day, enabling us gradually to gain control over the fierce passions that rage beneath the surface of consciousness in every one of us. Without an unbreakable will it is not possible to move up out of the Valley of the Shadow of Death which is our physical world. Untrained, the will becomes self-will, our worst enemy; but trained, the will can become our most powerful ally.

When on the bridge, the pilgrim says "Rama,
Rama," but afterwards, it's "Kama, Kama."

HINDU SAYING

Pilgrims traveling in the Himalayas sometimes
must cross deep ravines on rope bridges. While
on the bridge, which is swinging like a pendu-
lum, everyone says *"Rama, Rama, Rama,"*
"Lord, Lord, Lord," with as much devotion as
he or she can muster. But as soon as the first step
is taken on terra firma, it is likely to be *"Kama,*
Kama, Kama," "Pleasure, Pleasure, Pleasure."
When we are in the middle of turmoil we are very
responsive to the mantram; but as soon as our
health is good, our income is steady, and pleasures are flowing smoothly, we forget our Lord.

The Lord is a good psychologist: he knows
the way our minds run. Turmoil can be the
Lord's way of tapping us on the shoulder and
saying, "Don't forget me."

Love your enemies, bless them that curse you, do good to them that hate you.

THE GOSPEL ACCORDING TO
SAINT MATTHEW

This is love at its most magnificent. In order to love like this, we cannot be attached to ourselves. It is because we think so much about ourselves that we strike back, show resentment, speak harshly, move away.

Jesus' words do not mean agreeing with everything people say or supporting whatever they do. We sometimes have to oppose people we love. Yet, if we do it tenderly, it is not likely that it will cost us a single friend. In fact, that person may say, "I've found a friend who will support me and stand beside me through thick and thin."

The affairs of the world will go on forever.
Do not delay the practice of meditation.

MILAREPA

The human being simply does not have enough fuel in one lifetime to explore every byway that presents itself. If we had a thousand years to live, we could explore every roadside attraction, doing all the little things that appeal to us, and still have time left for realizing the goal of life. But even the most long-lived of us will be given a hundred years at most – and but a fraction of that time before vitality and resolution begin to wane.

People approach the spiritual life in one of two ways: there are the "locals" and the "express" trains. The "locals" stop at every little station along the way to sample the food and enjoy the local color. But the "express" goes straight through to the destination. Fortunately, there seems to be an inner law: we start as "locals" but become "expresses" as we make progress on our journey. When we take to meditation and put all our heart into practicing spiritual disciplines, we find ourselves speeding towards the goal.

*Grant what thou commandest
and then command what thou wilt.*

SAINT AUGUSTINE

Assessing his own inner resources and finding them meager, Augustine strikes a humble bargain with the Lord that has endeared him to spiritual aspirants down the ages. He says, "I'll do whatever you like, Lord. I'll overcome the most towering passion. But only if you make it possible."

It would be poor sportsmanship indeed if the Lord were to throw us into the arena of life, loose the lions upon us, and then leave us to our own devices. But this is not his way. When he sends us a temptation, he also grants the weapons with which to resist it. By moving closer to the Lord in meditation, by calling on him with his Holy Name, by striving to carry out all the disciplines that wise spiritual counselors have recommended through their own lives, we can gradually ally ourselves with the Lord so completely that we have access to everything that is his. We learn love without limit, courage without fail, wisdom that can penetrate the toughest problems life offers.

Unto every one that hath shall be given,
and he shall have abundance: but from him
that hath not shall be taken away
even that which he hath.

THE GOSPEL ACCORDING TO
SAINT MATTHEW

This is a strange paradox, a little-known secret. Jesus isn't speaking of worldly goods. He is speaking of a very rare kind of treasure: the more you draw on it, the more you will have. The more patient you are with people, for instance, the more patience you will have. The more generous you are today, the more generosity you will have tomorrow. The more love you give, the more loving you become.

The principle can be stated in the plainest of terms: if you are selfish with your love, the scant security you cling to will be battered to pieces by life. But if you give of yourself freely, your security will be unshakable. Your joy will be limitless. You will always have more to give.

An attitude to life which seeks fulfillment in the single-minded pursuit of wealth – in short, materialism – does not fit into this world, because it contains within itself no limiting principle, while the environment in which it is placed is strictly limited.

E.F. SCHUMACHER

The very air we breathe is not inexhaustible. San Francisco used to pity Los Angeles for its smog, yet today clean air in the Bay Area is the exception rather than the rule. In our beautiful city, there are days when children are asked to stay indoors because the air outside is so thick with smog – smog caused by greed.

If we love our children as we profess to, we should remember that the air is limited, exhaustible, a perishable member of the family of life. Treat it gently. Treat it with care. Don't blow fumes into the air or dump poisons into the rivers and oceans just because it increases profits. Don't fan overconsumption by buying things you do not need. It is not only corporations who carry the responsibility for pollution. Insofar as we tell them, "Produce all you want! We'll buy whatever you make," the rest of us are responsible too.

It is a wise commentator on today's world who points out that we do not inherit from our parents, we borrow from our children. Let us do all we can from today onwards to ensure that our children's children will live in a world unthreatened by radioactive waste and chemical pollution.

*The heart benevolent and kind
The most resembles God.*

ROBERT BURNS

When all is said and done, I doubt very much if any of us in the modern world is able to extinguish the fierce fire of self-will without the benefit of personal relationships. In a close relationship between man and woman, parent and child, or friend and friend, it is natural to want to put the other person first at least part of the time. I don't say it is easy. But it *is* natural and fulfilling, because the desire for unity is already there. You have something in common with the other person, so you can identify with him and find joy in contributing to her welfare.

People sometimes ask me, "How can we tell how to put somebody else first?" There is no special secret to this. You only need remember that what irritates you, irritates others. Nobody likes a joke at his expense. No one likes to be talked about behind her back. No one likes to be ignored when he says hello, or to be talked down to, or to be interrupted. Everybody is hurt by rudeness, agitated by being rushed or pressured. Being kind – that is the sum and substance of putting others first.

*Man must evolve for all human conflict a
method which rejects revenge, aggression
and retaliation. The foundation
of such a method is love.*

MARTIN LUTHER KING, JR.

All of us can play an important part in the conquest of violence. We can do this by throwing our full weight behind peaceful, effective programs for eliminating the situations from which violence arises. But just as importantly, we need to do everything we can to remove every trace of hostility in ourselves.

The violence that is flaring up on our streets and in many corners of the world is the inevitable expression of the hostility in our hearts. Hostility is like an infectious disease. Whenever we indulge in a violent act or even in hostile words, we are passing this disease on to those around us. When we quarrel at home, it is not just a domestic problem, we are contributing to turmoil everywhere.

A teacher of meditation in ancient India, Patanjali, wrote that in the presence of a man or woman in whom all hostility has died, others cannot be hostile. In the presence of a man or woman in whom all fear has died, no one can be afraid. This is the power released in true nonviolence, as we can see in the life of Mahatma Gandhi. Because all hostility had died in his heart, he was a profound force for peace.

Give a little love to a child,
and you get a great deal back.
JOHN RUSKIN

Those who have children can become masters of patience, endurance, and steadfastness, because children will test you at every turn. Little ones are ruthless observers. When I see a five-year-old watching me, I feel as though Sherlock Holmes is on my track. I can almost hear him saying, "Elementary, my dear Mr. Watson. I can see the inconsistency between his word and deed quite clearly." The way to make our children patient and loving is to be that way ourselves. When we are provoked, most of us get agitated, and it is then that we need to repeat the mantram. By continually calling on the Lord, who is the source of strength within us, we can make our lives an inspiring example to our children.

*Even as a tortoise draws in its limbs,
the wise can draw in their senses at will.*

SRI KRISHNA (BHAGAVAD GITA)

Sri Krishna says a free person can draw in his senses just as a tortoise draws in its legs. What a marvelous simile! Just imagine a tortoise being approached by a group of school children with sticks in their hands. He sees the children coming, and the command is given to the limbs, "Retire!" Immediately, the head, the tail, and the four legs withdraw into the shell. The children come; they beat out a rhythm on the shell with their sticks. They toss the tortoise in the air, but they can't harm him.

After the children leave and all is quiet, the tortoise ventures to stick his neck out, then his tail and legs. He continues his journey, unconcerned. He goes where he likes.

If we want to live in freedom, Krishna says, we must train our senses. We learn when to welcome an experience, and when to withdraw for our own safety. We become masters of our lives. Then we will be like the giant tortoise I saw at the zoo – wandering freely while all the other animals were in cages. A notice on his back read: "I am free. Don't report me to the management."

*As you repeat the Holy Name, gather
quietly, little by little, your thoughts and
feelings and will around it; gather around it
your whole being. Let the name penetrate
your soul as a drop of oil spreads out and
penetrates a cloth. Let nothing of yourself
escape. Surrender your whole self and
enclose it within the Name.*

ON THE INVOCATION OF THE
NAME OF JESUS

The little waits and delays that life is so full of are all opportunities to repeat the mantram. In the morning, when you're waiting for the coffee to perk, you can repeat the mantram instead of staring blankly at the wall. When you are standing in line at the bank or the supermarket, the mantram will make the wait seem shorter, and your patience will help those around you too. When you are waiting for an interview, or for the doctor to come in, the mantram can save you a good deal of anxiety.

In all these cases, you are putting your time to better use than if you were just letting your mind run on about what might be troubling it. You are saving yourself from unnecessary tension and anxiety. You are sending the mantram deeper into your consciousness.

It is many of these little moments that finally add up to tremendous spiritual growth. Patience and concentration blossom in the space that you have cleared for them.

We may make an oratory of our heart
wherein to retire from time to time to
converse with Him in meekness, humility,
and love. Every one is capable of such
familiar conversation with God,
some more, some less. He
knows what we can do.
Let us begin, then.

BROTHER LAWRENCE

Still your mind in me, still your intellect in
me, and without doubt you will be united
with me forever. If you cannot still your
mind in me, learn to do so through the
regular practice of meditation.

SRI KRISHNA (BHAGAVAD GITA)

Meditation is the basis of the spiritual life. It is meditation that enables us to understand the teachings of the mystics and apply them in our daily life. It is meditation that gives us the immense power to stay patient and forgiving when all our conditioning is crying out for retaliation. There is nothing glamorous about meditation. It is a lot of hard, hard work. But when you know from your own experience what the tremendous benefits can be, you look forward to meditation. When the alarm goes off in the morning, even in the dead of winter when the bed is warm and the blankets hold you down, you get up for your meditation with eagerness and enthusiasm every day, well or not so well, because you know that meditation is the key to the art of living.

*Each day is a little life; every waking and
rising a little birth; every fresh morning
a little youth; every going to rest
and sleep a little death.*

ARTHUR SCHOPENHAUER

My grandmother, my spiritual teacher, used to tell me that the pain we associate with the great change called death arises from our innumerable selfish attachments. One day she illustrated this in a simple way by asking me to sit in a chair and hold tight to the arms. Then she tried to pull me out of the chair. She tugged and pulled at me, and I held on tight. It was painful. She was a strong person, and even though I held on with all my strength, she pulled me out.

Then she told me to sit down again, but this time not to hold on anywhere – just to get up and come to her when she called. With ease I got out of the chair and went to her. This, she told me, is how to overcome the fear and pain of death. When we hold onto things – houses, cars, books, guitars, our antique silver teapot – we get attached and tied down.

*Do not you believe that there is in man a
deep so profound as to be hidden
even to him in whom it is?*

SAINT AUGUSTINE

In talking about deeper levels of consciousness, metaphors can be helpful. So let's talk about the "lake of the mind." It is a deep lake, but we are familiar only with the surface. We know how to swim effortlessly on the surface; modern life is quite good at teaching us all kinds of ingenious strokes for this. It even supplies us with flotation devices that keep us bouncing pleasurably on the surface of life forever.

Yet over time we become aware of how much distress is involved in the struggle merely to stay afloat. For some reason, peace of mind simply doesn't seem attainable; the mind keeps stirring up a never-ending succession of waves.

Life on the shimmering surface of consciousness, we are someday forced to admit, isn't everything it's supposed to be. We come to the uncomfortable realization that there is simply no guarantee of security anywhere as long as we're living on the surface of life. At some point, every sensitive person is ready to dive – deep into consciousness in meditation. He or she wants to find out whether something more reliable lies below. Often it is the spiritual teacher who gives us the courage to dive. We ask ourselves, "If he has done it, why can't I?"

*Whoever approaches Me walking, I will
come to him running; and he who meets Me
with sins equivalent to the whole world, I
will greet him with forgiveness equal to it.*

MISHKAT AL-MASABAIH

*When we take one step toward God,
he takes seven steps toward us.*

HINDU PROVERB

In the Hindu scriptures, it is often said that the
Lord wants nothing more than that we should all
be united with him. He is very eager to see us
take the first step, but he knows us very well by
now: he watches carefully to see that we take
that step and do not wobble back and forth. It is
not enough just to put your foot forward and
touch it lightly to the ground; you must put your
weight on it completely. When we do take that
step – by bearing patiently with those around
us, or by changing some unhealthy habit, or by
repeating the Holy Name – we can be sure that
he will take seven steps toward us. But we must
take the first step.

Man is not holier or higher for the outward works that he does. Truly God that is the Beholder of the heart rewards the will more than the deed. The deeds truly hang on the will, not the will on the deeds.

RICHARD ROLLE

It is because we don't have any real challenge in life that most of us do not grow to our real height. We need a challenge that is worthy of our capacities, and making money, if I may say so, is not much of a challenge. Neither is becoming famous or achieving power; and as for pleasure, challenge is conspicuous by its absence.

But becoming rich in personal relationships, learning to return love for hatred, being always aware of the unity of life, these things are the most difficult achievements on the face of the earth. Only when we see a person who has accomplished such feats do we begin to glimpse the heights a human being can attain. This is our real stature, and no matter what our problems or liabilities, every one of us can attain these heights through the regular, enthusiastic practice of meditation.

*By love I do not mean any natural
tenderness, which is more or less in people
according to their constitution; but I mean a
larger principle of the soul, founded in reason
and piety, which makes us tender, kind and
gentle to all our fellow creatures as creatures
of God, and for his sake.*

WILLIAM LAW

Behind sexual desire is a very natural longing
that is not altogether physical: the longing to escape the loneliness of separate existence. It always surprises people when I say that those who
have strong passions should congratulate themselves. They have a lot of gas in their tank, a lot
of vital energy in reserve. But gas is to be used,
not drained; if you let your car sit with a hole in
the tank, you are likely to be out of fuel when
you need it most. The stronger a person's sexual
desire, the more vital it is that the power behind
these desires be harnessed.

When we begin to transform the passion of
sex, we will find a gentleness and tenderness entering into all our relationships. The most romantic relationships are not really based on
sexual attraction – they are based on tenderness
and respect for one another.

In vain our labours are, whatsoe'er they be,
Unless God gives the Benedicite.

ROBERT HERRICK

The spiritual life is a call to action. But it is a call to *selfless* action, that is, action without any selfish attachment to the results. It is not action or effort that we must surrender; it is self-will, and this is terribly difficult. You must do your best constantly, yet never allow yourself to become involved in whether things work out the way you want.

It takes many years of practice to learn this skill, but once you have it, you will never lose your nerve. The sense of inadequacy goes. You are able to assess your capacities with detachment. You choose a worthwhile goal, then you can throw yourself into selfless action without conflict or diffidence or fatigue. When we learn simply to do our best and leave the question of success or failure to the Lord, the results can really be spectacular.

*Suffering is the ancient law of love; there is
no quest without pain; there is no lover
who is not also a martyr.*

HEINRICH SUSO

Practically speaking, in order to learn to love,
we need a tool for transforming anger into compassion, resentment into sympathy. We need
some kind of brake to apply when the mind
shifts into high gear under the influence of anger
and other negative emotions. The mind is so
used to having its own way in almost everything,
that all it knows is how to race out of control.

How many of you would ever step into your
Pontiac or Toyota if you knew the brake could
suddenly fail? I could say, "You have plenty of
gas, a big engine, gorgeous upholstery, radial
tires, eight-channel stereo tape deck, ashtray.
Why don't you go ahead?" You would reply,
"But I can't stop the thing!" The vast majority of
us, amazingly enough, manage to travel through
life without knowing how to brake the engine of
the mind.

We can all install a simple but effective brake,
the mantram. Whenever you feel agitated, annoyed, impolite, or downright angry, keep repeating the mantram. Gradually the mind will
race less and less. When the brake is thoroughly
road-tested, you will have the equipment to be
patient and kind in every situation. You will be
ready to face the tests that real love demands.

*He that is slow to anger is better than the
mighty; and he that ruleth his spirit
than he that taketh a city.*

PROVERBS

In the interest of good health, in the interest of a
long life, in the interest of loving relationships, it
is essential to learn how to deal with our anger
creatively and constructively. If we do not, in
time it will no longer be isolated outbursts of
anger; we will become the victims of an unending stream of rage, seething just below the surface of life, with which no human being can
cope.

Through meditation and the mantram or
Holy Name, however, every one of us can learn
to reduce the speed of our thinking, and install a
reliable speedometer in our mind. Then, whenever the speed of thinking goes over, say, fifty-
five, one of those recorded voices will automatically whisper, "Be careful. You may not be able
to keep your car on the road."

Positive thoughts travel slowly, leisurely.
The slow mind is clear, kind, and efficient; in the
beautiful phrase of the Bible, it is "slow to
wrath." Patience means thoughts puttering
along like Sunday drivers, taking the trouble to
notice the needs of people around.

*Thou wast seeking what thou shouldest offer
in thy behalf; offer thyself. For what doth
God ask of thee, except thyself? Since in the
whole earthly creation He made
nothing better than thee.*

SAINT AUGUSTINE

The scriptures of all religions have a great deal to say about renunciation. They are not asking us to renounce our stamp collection or our tickets to the World Series; they are asking us to sacrifice our self-will. Reducing self-will is a terribly painful renunciation to make, because the ego will try every trick in the book to undermine our efforts.

Just as the mountain climber does not begin with Mount Everest, you cannot get rid of all your self-will immediately. Practically speaking, it is best to start on a very small scale. When you go out to dinner with a friend, instead of painstakingly choosing just what you like, have what the other person is having. More likely than not it will be something you would just as soon pass over. That is the time to smile and enjoy it. If two people who care deeply about one another can do this, can learn to like what the person they love likes, they have gotten a little of their self-will out of the way. They cannot help moving closer to each other.

*A tree is known by its fruit; a man by his
deeds. A good deed is never lost; he who sows
courtesy reaps friendship, and he who
plants kindness gathers love.*

SAINT BASIL

I am the first to admit that it takes a lot of endurance to put the other person first, especially when your efforts seem to be met with indifference. When you start giving another person your best, especially in an emotionally entangled relationship, he may not notice it for weeks. This kind of indifference can really sting. You want to go up to him, tap him on the shoulder, and say, "Hello, Thomas, I've just been kind to you." Thomas would say, "Oh, thank you, I didn't even know it" – not because he was trying to be rude, but because he was preoccupied with himself.

To be patient and go on giving your best, you can't have expectations about how other people are going to respond. You can't afford to ask, "Does he *like* me? I've been putting him first for two whole weeks, and I don't think he even cares." What does it matter? If you go on putting him first, you're growing. You're learning how to rub off the edges and corners that make human relationships difficult. You are becoming the kind of person that everyone wants to be with, that everyone admires and feels comfortable with.

God has created the world in play.

SRI RAMAKRISHNA

A simple, childlike story in India's ancient
scriptures tells how multiplicity emerged from
unity. The Lord, the One without a second, felt
very lonesome one morning. After all, he was
the only thing that existed in the entire universe,
so when he looked around him, he could see no
one but himself. This did not satisfy him at all.
He wanted to play.

So he made playmates. Out of himself he created the myriads of creatures, the two-footed
and the four-footed. He started playing with
them, playing hide-and-seek, which is what life
is all about. We are all playing this game with the
Lord. We are all seeking him, and he is hiding
playfully from us.

It is easy to talk about this, sing about this,
paint this, but it is an entirely different matter to
experience it – to see Krishna, or Christ, or the
Buddha masquerading in this world. Yet in
deepest meditation, the veil separating you and
me can drop. Then, beneath the varied cos-
tumes, we will be able to perceive the same supreme Reality whom we call God, who is playing his game in the world.

Pray without ceasing.
In every thing give thanks.

I THESSALONIANS

Each creature has its being
from the One Name,
From which it comes forth,
And to which it returns,
With praises unending.

SHABISTARI

Instead of saying the mantram once, the way we say hello at the beginning of a conversation, the idea is to repeat it over and over again. The effect of the mantram is cumulative. With constant repetition, constant practice, it takes root in our consciousness and gradually transforms it. This may sound tedious, but it is far from that. The mantram soon becomes a familiar friend of whom we never grow tired.

*We must not wish anything other than
what happens from moment to moment,
all the while, however, exercising
ourselves in goodness.*

SAINT CATHERINE OF GENOA

A tremendous amount of our vital energy is squandered in the vacillations of the mind. If things go our way, we get elated; if things do not go our way, we get depressed. Yet elation and depression are made from the same cloth.

It is when the mind is getting elated that we need to be very vigilant, because what goes up will inevitably come down. If, through the practice of meditation and repetition of the mantram, we can keep the mind calm when good things are coming our way, then when bad things come, we won't be depressed. Our mind will stay calm.

Only then will we be free to be truly spontaneous in our responses to life.

*Meditation brings wisdom; lack of
meditation leaves ignorance. Know well
what leads you forward and what holds
you back, and choose the path
that leads to wisdom.*

THE BUDDHA

Blaming ourselves when we get angry is not going to be of much help in the long run. What is helpful is to gain a clearer understanding of how anger comes about. Getting angry is like having a malfunctioning engine. The mind is like the engine of the body, which can be compared to the chassis of the car we drive. But the sad fact is that most of us know a lot more about our car engine than we do about our own minds.

We don't even have the slightest idea of where the ignition switch of the mind is located. As a result, the engine goes on cranking out thoughts of every description throughout the day and throughout the long night in dreams. Worry and resentment and anger use up enormous quantities of vitality. It's like leaving our car idling in the garage all night long; in the morning when we need to get to work, we have to push it down the road.

What we need to do is learn how to slow down the mind, and eventually to park it at the side of the road when travel isn't necessary. Then we will have all the vitality, all the fuel, we need when we want to reach a worthwhile destination.

A human being fashions his consequences
as surely as he fashions his goods or his
dwelling. Nothing that he says, thinks
or does is without consequences.

NORMAN COUSINS

The Hindu and Buddhist scriptures give us the same truth in what is called the law of karma, which is the psychological equivalent to the physical law that every action has a reaction equal and opposite to it. The Buddha says we can fly higher than the heavens or hide in the bowels of the earth, but we will not be able to escape the consequences of our actions. Though we drive to another city or fly to another country, though we change our job or our name, our mistakes will pursue us wherever we go.

Paradoxically, the only way we can begin to escape from the consequences of our actions is to stop running from them and to face them with fortitude. In this sense, every difficult situation is a precious opportunity. When we find ourselves in some situation where we always make the same mistake, if we can manage *not* to make that mistake, the chain can be broken. Often, if we face it squarely, that situation will not come up again.

Set me free from evil passions, and heal my
heart of all inordinate affections; that being
inwardly cured and thoroughly cleansed,
I may be made fit to love, courageous
to suffer, steady to persevere.

THOMAS A KEMPIS

At international airports today, every effort is
made to eliminate dangerous traveling companions: you and I have to make the same careful in-
quiries where powerful emotions are concerned. The fellow behind dark glasses, with the
folded newspaper under his arm – look out!
Interpol has a fat file on him. Don't take him
with you! The most ruthless hijackers can't hold
us hostage more effectively than our own passions – anger, fear, and lust – when they take
over our lives.

You can gradually learn to "dis-identify"
yourself from powerful negative emotions that
can turn on you. Once you can pull back from
anger or greed and say, "That's not really me,"
you've as good as snatched the hijacker's
weapon right out of his hands. Through the
practice of meditation, you can begin to choose
the thoughts and passions you wish to have as
companions on your journey through life.

*God is not external to anyone, but
is present with all things, though
they are ignorant that He is so.*

PLOTINUS

I have heard people claim that mysticism denies the physical world. A good mystic would answer, "We are not belittling Sir Isaac Newton. We don't deny the Pythagorean theorem. All we are saying is that we have discovered another dimension to life, another realm – changeless, eternal, beyond cause and effect – on which the entire physical universe rests."

Because our lives are so utterly oriented outward, we may doubt the existence of the Self within. I have been telling people about this Self almost daily for more than twenty years, but occasionally I still am asked, "Are you talking about something outside us?" Compared with this Self – whom we call Krishna or Christ, Allah or Adonai or the Divine Mother – my own body is "outside." Compared with the Self, my own life is not more dear.

*By faithfulness we are collected and bound
up into unity within ourselves, whereas we
had been scattered abroad in multiplicity.*

SAINT AUGUSTINE

Sensory pleasures are only nickel-and-dime satisfactions. It is only when we don't have a wider frame of reference that we believe they hold out the promise of great pleasure. When we widen our horizons to encompass a greater breadth of life, we can evaluate these pleasures more shrewdly.

Some of the greatest mystics experimented with their senses rather freely in their earlier days. Augustine himself admits to having painted ancient Carthage red. But when the mystics reach a state of unlimited compassion and concern for others, they admit, "Those were mere pennies. Now I am in possession of wealth beyond my wildest dreams."

Love makes everything that is heavy light.
THOMAS A KEMPIS

It is love that teaches us our real stature and reveals the heroism we never thought we possessed. The renunciation that might be well-nigh impossible in a vacuum can be blessedly simple when someone we love stands to gain. Turning down a second glass of wine might take some doing in ordinary circumstances, for example; but when you're in the company of an impressionable teenager, you'll gladly set it aside.

Suppose you're tempted to add to your collection of antique fire screens: hard to resist, maybe, if your aim is *solely* to reduce your own acquisitiveness. But if the money you save can be spent on a tent for family camping trips, it can be a breeze. You feel so good inside! A knack for quiet self-sacrifice is the very life and soul of friendship. Reducing self-will needn't be a joyless deprivation – it can be so many little acts of love, performed over and over throughout the day.

How poor are they that have not patience!
What wound did ever heal but by degrees?

WILLIAM SHAKESPEARE

Adopt the pace of nature,
her secret is patience.

RALPH WALDO EMERSON

Poets like to write about love, popular singers like to glorify love, but nobody bothers to sing the praises of patience. I once heard of a man who prayed to God, "Give me patience, O Lord, and give it to me now!" That man was not born with a patient nature. Most of us aren't – but we can develop it through practice.

You will find opportunities every day if you look for them. In a situation where there is a lot of friction, where people differ from you and aren't shy about letting you know it, don't run away. Move closer to them. You may have to grit your teeth; you may have to bite your lip to keep from giving vent to a harsh retort. And then of course you need to smile too, which doesn't come easily with your lip between your teeth. It is a demanding art to do this gracefully. But it is an art that can be learned with the help of the mantram.

*The senses have been conditioned by
attraction to the pleasant and aversion to the
unpleasant: a man should not be ruled by
them; they are obstacles in his path.*

SRI KRISHNA (BHAGAVAD GITA)

We are conditioned to like some things and to dislike others. There is not necessarily any logic to it – it is often just a matter of habit.

Take food, for example. We like what we learn to like. In Kerala we have a particular kind of mango that is eaten green, when it is acutely sour. There is nothing inherently pleasant about this sensation; in fact, a detached observer would call it painful. But everybody likes it; everybody eats it; so you learn to like it too. And in the end, you cannot do without it.

Beneath all likes and dislikes is a basic compulsion of the mind to pass judgment on everything: "I like this, I don't like that." When this compulsion is rigid, it is rigid everywhere – with food, with philosophies, and especially with other people.

So, when we free ourselves from a compulsive liking for sour green mangos – or chocolate cake or red chilis – the whole likes-and-dislikes compulsion is weakened. As a result, all our other likes and dislikes will have a looser hold on us, giving us greater freedom, which will affect even our personal relationships for the better.

*Lord, how can I ever find rest anywhere else
when I am made to find rest in thee?*

SAINT AUGUSTINE

The vast majority of human beings spend their lives in the pursuit of cherished goals which, when they are achieved, often leave them even more restless and unfulfilled. There is nothing wrong with desire. Like electricity, which can light a home or electrocute the tenant, desire is neither good nor bad. It is the most powerful force we have to drive us to action. Tragedy comes when desire is not subject either to the intellect or to the conscious will. Then we have a powerful vehicle speeding without anybody in the driver's seat.

Imagine all the cars in your home town coming out of their garages and going about anywhere they like without drivers. How many accidents there would be, how much damage to life and property! When I go after what I desire, and you do the same, sooner or later we collide.

We need to learn to distinguish between purely personal goals and those that include the happiness of other people. These latter desires provide a more lasting fuel for our actions, and lead to the kind of fulfillment that doesn't fade.

Love consists not in feeling great things
but in having great detachment
and in suffering for the Beloved.

SAINT JOHN OF THE CROSS

In *My Fair Lady*, Rex Harrison sings in exasperation: "Why can't a woman be more like a man? . . . / Why can't a woman be like *me*?" It did not surprise me to learn that this was a very popular song. In every emotional relationship, even if we don't put it into words, each of us has a rigid set of expectations which requires the other person to act and think in a particular way. Interestingly enough, it is not *that* person's way; it is our own.

When he or she acts differently, we get surprised and feel irritated or disappointed. If we could see behind the scenes, in the mind, this sort of encounter would make a good comedy. Here I am, relating not to you but to my idea of you, and I get irritated because you insist on acting your own way instead!

It is really no more than stimulus and response. If you behave the way I expect, the way I want, I'll be kind. If you behave otherwise, I'll act otherwise too: rude or irritated or disappointed or depressed, depending on my personality, but always something in reaction to you. It means, simply, that none of us has much freedom; our behavior is dependent on what other people say and do. To live without self-centered expectations is the secret of freedom in personal relationships.

*Trifles make perfection
and perfection is no trifle.*
MICHELANGELO

To lead the spiritual life, we need not play a part on a gigantic scale. Mogul art, one of the great periods of artistic achievement in India, often is in miniature. The artist concentrated on very small areas, on little things, and worked with tenderness and precision. Only somebody who understands art will be able to see all the love and labor that has gone into it. Family living is like Mogul art, worked in miniature. The canvas is so small, and the skill required is so great, that most of us really do not appreciate the vast potentialities of family life.

Today we hear a great deal about the family becoming obsolete. Let us hope this is just the fantasy of those who do not understand the value of the family. To me, the family is like a free university, where we can get our finest education in living for others. Family does not just mean Papa, Mama, Junior, and Janie, but all the members, including grandparents, uncles and aunts and country cousins. The family can include dear friends and those who participate closely in all our endeavors.

We begin by being tender and unselfish and putting up with innumerable discomforts for the sake of adding to the joy of our family. Then, gradually, we extend our love to include our friends, our community, our country, and our world.

The main reason for the invisible God
incarnating himself physically in the midst
of human beings was to lead them who can
love only physically to the healthy love of
his physical appearance, and then,
little by little, to spiritual love.

SAINT BERNARD

When we meditate on the Lord, we are meditating on a visible symbol of the huge reservoir of love each of us has trapped deep within himself or herself. It is the embodied example of this love to which we are looking for inspiration when we meditate on Jesus' perfect love for his Father in the Lord's Prayer, on Sri Krishna as the perfect friend and spiritual guide in the Bhagavad Gita, and on Sri Ramakrishna's childlike devotion to the Divine Mother in his beautiful hymns. Our personal devotion to one of these ideals of love deepens immensely as a natural course of events when we are meditating ardently and carrying out the allied disciplines to the best of our ability.

*No man hath so cordial a feeling of the
Passion of Christ, as he who hath
suffered the like himself.*

THOMAS A KEMPIS

The principle underlying the Passion of Christ
is that out of his infinite mercy, the Lord has
taken our suffering upon himself. As long as any
living creature is in pain, so is Jesus, for he lives
at the heart of all. Wherever violence breaks out,
no matter how cleverly we try to justify it, we are
crucifying the spirit of Christ.

Patience and *passion* both come from a Latin
word meaning to suffer or endure. When we
speak of the Passion of Christ, we are recalling
the suffering he endured on the cross. Whenever
we practice patience – cheerfully bearing with
somebody who is irascible, or enduring discomfort
rather than imposing it on others – in a
small way we are embracing the principle of the
Passion.

This does not mean becoming blind to what
others are doing. I know when somebody is
being rude or unkind, but it does not impair my
faith in that person. I keep my eyes on the core of
goodness in him; and I act towards her as I
would have her act towards me. There is only
one way to make others more loving, and that is
by loving more ourselves.

*Just as a flower gives out its fragrance to
whomsoever approaches or uses it, so love
from within us radiates towards everybody
and manifests as spontaneous service.*

SWAMI RAMDAS

Many of us find it difficult to be compassionate
towards other people for the simple reason that
most of our sensitivity is directed towards ourselves. The less we dwell on ourselves, the more
our sensitivity will open out to the needs and
feelings of others.

Every time you hurt someone and then grieve
inside because of it, you are attending a valuable
seminar on sensitivity. It is a seminar at the deepest and most personal level, the experiential, and
it is infinitely more effective than anything we
can attend for college credit. The credit comes to
us directly, when we change our behavior and
don't hurt people again. "Everybody's feelings
can be hurt," we realize, "just like my own. I
have to take others' feelings into consideration
in what I do."

When meditation is mastered,
the mind is unwavering like the flame
of a lamp in a windless place.

SRI KRISHNA (BHAGAVAD GITA)

The spirit of man is the candle of the Lord.

PROVERBS

Clay lamps are still used today in India, where they are lit and placed in an alcove of the shrine. Since there is no wind in the protected niche, the tongue of the flame burns without a flicker.

In the depths of your meditation, when you are concentrating on an inspirational passage such as the Prayer of Saint Francis, your mind will be like the tongue of flame in a windless place – motionless and steady. At that time you will be concentrating completely on the words of the prayer, which means that you are slowly becoming like Saint Francis in your daily conduct and consciousness. It requires enormous endeavor to do this, but through ceaseless effort every one of us can reach the state in which the mind, like the flame of the clay lamp, does not flicker or waver at all.

The knower and the known are one. Simple
people imagine that they should see God, as
if He stood there and they here. This is not so.
God and I, we are one in knowledge.

MEISTER ECKHART

In order to say that there is no one in our deeper
consciousness, we have to go there, knock on
the door, and find that no one is at home. Until
he has made that journey, knocked on the door,
and heard a voice saying "There is no one here,"
no one should call himself an atheist. Agnostic is
more correct.

Of those who tell me they are atheists, I ask,
"Don't you believe in yourself?"

Their answer is, "Of course."

"Then," I say, "you believe in God."

When we use terms like "God" or "Lord" it is
not referring to someone "out there." We are in-
voking someone who is inside us all the time,
who is nearer to us than our body, dearer to us
than our life.

When I was a child, I spake as a child, I
understood as a child, I thought as a child:
but when I became a man
I put away childish things.

I CORINTHIANS

I have sometimes heard adults, who should show more wisdom, complaining, "I want all the pleasures of the senses I enjoyed in my teens." I would like to put before them the example of my young friend Jessica. It wasn't very long ago that I saw her playing with dolls. I understand there are dolls now which, if you press a button, actually get a fever. Perfect for playing hospital! But Jess has graduated from dolls to people. She has worked hard to become an accomplished nurse, and now she is helping and comforting real patients. She also has two beautiful children of her own. Of course, she no longer has any need for dolls.

In the same way, now that we are grown up, our joy should consist in helping others. Once we so much as taste this joy, we will feel no need to play at being children again.

He is not the same, nor is he another.

THE BUDDHA

The Buddha is saying that we change from moment to moment. Personality is not cast in a rigid mold; the whole secret of personality is that it is a process.

The nature of a process is that it can be changed. For a time, it is true, the changes you are trying to make will not seem natural. When someone is rude to you, you will still feel a wave of resentment inside. It does not matter; at the outset, it is enough to *act* kind, to pretend to be kind, to stage a sort of kindness performance.

Gradually, if you put your whole effort behind this transformation, and meditate with diligence, the seething will subside. Then it will not just be a flawless performance, you will actually transform anger into compassion. You will feel sorry for the person who has offended you. You will not be the same angry person you used to be; and yet you will not be someone else, either. To be patient, kind, and secure is our real nature; anything else is being false to ourselves.

Be ye kind one to another, tenderhearted,
forgiving one another, even as God for
Christ's sake hath forgiven you.

EPHESIANS

Often it is nothing more than our likes and dislikes that keep us from seeing the core of purity and selflessness that is in everyone. We don't like the way he cuts his hair, we don't like the way she drops her *r*'s, and we can't get beyond these surface obstacles. Yet if we free ourselves from the rigid dictates of our own likes and dislikes, we will see people more clearly – even those whom we find difficult to love.

This is seldom easy. Some people *are* a little more irritating and self-willed than others. But instead of criticizing such people, which only makes their alienation worse, we can focus all our attention on what is best in them. This most practical skill can help those around us tremendously – while it helps us get over our likes and dislikes as well. It is like turning a flashlight onto one particular spot, concentrating on what is kind, generous, and selfless in the other person. We'll find that this kind of support draws out and strengthens these very qualities in him or her.

It doesn't much signify whom one marries,
for one is sure to find out the next morning
that it was someone else.

SAMUEL ROGERS

All, everything that I understand,
I understand only because I love.

LEO TOLSTOY

There is nothing easy about learning to love. The real romantic must be very practical: it takes a lot of hard, unromantic work to sustain any human relationship. Naturally there are going to be differences between you and your partner. Identical twins have differences of opinion, so why should two people from, say, New York City and Paris, Texas, expect life together to be smooth sailing?

Even on the honeymoon there may be difficulties. You open Pandora's box expecting a lot of doves and out come a couple of bats instead. You have to be ready to say, "The doves are there; they're simply lying low. Why don't we get to work and shoo away these bats?" Rather than dwelling on the negative, try to respect the potential in the other person and help him or her to realize that potential through your support. If you want a relationship to get deeper and deeper with the passage of time, you will go on strengthening it all your life.

*In order to overcome our desires and to
renounce all those things, our love and
inclination for which are wont so to inflame
the will that it delights therein, we require
a more ardent fire and a nobler love –
that of the Bridegroom.*

SAINT JOHN OF THE CROSS

Most of us are not aware to what extent our desires are compulsive. We do not realize how often they push and shove us about without any say on our part. But when we think "*I* would like a hot fudge sundae," it would be more accurate to say that the desire is thinking *us*. Intellectually we may know that a hot fudge sundae means more calories than we need; but the desire has a hold on us, and we believe, temporarily, this is what will satisfy us. Not until we have eaten the sundae do we reflect, "That's not what I *really* wanted. Why did I go and eat it?"

Not that there is anything wrong in eating sundaes. The important point is that we do not have the capacity to *choose*. For "hot fudge sundae" we can substitute our own favorite pleasures. Some may not be harmful in themselves, but when the inability to choose extends to destructive habits such as smoking, drinking, or taking drugs, we begin to cause suffering to ourselves and to those around us.

Manifest plainness,
Embrace simplicity,
Reduce selfishness,
Have few desires.

LAO-TZU

Detachment from likes and dislikes, habits and opinions, is not a sign of weakness. It is an enormously strong and positive quality. Nor does freedom from likes and dislikes mean that life is insipid for us, but rather that we are not driven compulsively by rigid ways of thinking. Even if we don't get what we want – or if we do get what we don't want – we can still function cheerfully and efficiently.

Detachment from habits does not mean that we have no habits. Good habits can be very useful to cultivate in life. But we should be able to change our habits gracefully, or drop them altogether when necessary, especially if we learn that they are harmful to us or are not exactly endearing us to those around us. If we are used to a cup of coffee every morning with our breakfast and one morning we discover that we are out of coffee, we don't say, "I can't function without my coffee," and go back to bed. We should be able to say cheerfully, "I'll have tea instead, or better still, soy milk."

Let me not to the marriage of true minds
Admit impediments. Love is not love
Which alters when it alteration finds,
Or bends with the remover to remove.

WILLIAM SHAKESPEARE

Many of the disruptions that take place in personal relationships can be prevented by learning to control our attention, for attention is closely linked with loyalty.

I can illustrate with that most fascinating of relationships, the romantic. Suppose *Romeo and Juliet* had turned out differently, and the two lovers had married and settled down to a normal domestic life. After a few years, as sometimes happens, Romeo's attention gets restless. Once the very sight of Juliet made him think of flowers and bubbling brooks and the "light, sweet airs of spring"; now she just reminds him of the laundry and his morning espresso. After a while, his attention falls on Rosalind, his old flame. Now *she* reminds him of flowers and brooks; his attention grabs on to her and will not let go.

Today, Romeo would most likely receive the advice, "Follow your desires. That is where happiness will be." But that is just where *un*-happiness will be. If Romeo's attention cannot stay with Juliet, how is it going to stay with Rosalind? If he cannot get control over his attention, happiness can only recede farther and farther.

*He that loveth, flieth, runneth, and
rejoiceth. He is free, and cannot be held in.
He giveth all for all, and hath all in all,
because he resteth in one highest above
all things, from whom all that is
good flows and proceeds.*

THOMAS A KEMPIS

This spring I watched six baby swallows learn how to fly. They were huddled on the telephone wires observing their mother, who came flying slowly by in front of them, doing the easier turns and showing them the basics of flying. There was no need for these baby swallows to read books or attend lectures on how to fly. They have an inborn instinct for it. Learning to fly may not be easy, but this is what birds are born to do.

The Lord sees us sitting on a perch made of pleasure, profit, power, or prestige, quaking with every variation in our bank account and every critical comment that comes our way; and he asks us if we would not rather forget our failings, weaknesses, and insecurities and become united with him.

This is what we are born to do: to leave our perch of selfish interests and soar aloft. To soar to union with God means to give all our love to the Lord, so that all the faculties and resources which have been hidden in us can come into our lives to the great benefit of those around us.

As the hart panteth after the water brooks,
so panteth my soul after thee, O Lord.

PSALMS

After years of meditation, the Lord may reveal himself to us in some small measure. Then we shall see into the very heart of life. This vision may last for only a moment or two, but it leaves behind an unforgettable awareness of the living presence of the Lord.

Once we have tasted the joy of this experience, the ordinary pleasures of life become insipid in comparison. All our desires will be unified around one great desire to recapture this experience. When this great longing comes to us, the Divine Fisherman has got his hook into us forever. Doesn't Eckhart, the German mystic, say that the more we thrash about, the deeper the hook enters? We may try to run away, to do everything we can think of to get free; but finally, when we get a glimpse of who it is who has caught us, we realize what a blessing it is to be caught so firmly by the Lord.

"This is myself and this is another."
Be free of this bond which
encompasses you about.
And your own self is thereby released.

SARAHA

To love completely, it is not enough if I care deeply; I must also be detached from myself. To know what is best for someone, I have to be able to step aside from my own prejudices and preconceptions, slip into that person's shoes, and become one with him temporarily, looking at life through his eyes rather than my own. When I step back again, I will have seen his needs from the inside; only then can I see clearly how to serve those needs with detachment and compassion.

Why, then, do we find it so desperately difficult to get ourselves out of the way? The reason, the mystics reply, is that we live rather superficially, on the surface of life. On the surface, we feel that it is natural for people to quarrel, for nations to go to war. "It's only human," we say. Only in the depths of the soul can we realize that quarreling and fighting are not natural at all. What is natural is loving everybody, seeing everybody as one.

And this is happiness, to be joyful in Thee and for Thee and because of Thee, this and no other. Those who think happiness is any other, pursue a joy that is apart from Thee and is no true joy. . . . Why are they not happy? Because they are much more concerned over things which are more powerful to make them unhappy than truth is to make them happy, in that they remember truth so slightly.

SAINT AUGUSTINE

If someone were to pull over to the side of the road in San Francisco and ask me how to get to Los Angeles, I wouldn't say, "Go north." Everyone knows you have to go in the other direction. Similarly, spiritual figures like Saint Augustine tell us, "Don't follow your selfish desires and angry impulses; that is the way to emotional bankruptcy." But we reply, "Oh, no! I know what I'm doing."

Saint Augustine would insist, "Please believe me. If you go that way, you will become more insecure. Instead, let me show you a secret trail that will take you slowly round to security."

The route is always there and it is always open. We must be prepared for many years of arduous hiking over rough terrain. Very likely we are going to have lapses; some attractive detours may distract us temporarily. All that we should ask for is the determination to do our best to stay on the right trail and go forward.

*Mind is consciousness which has
put on limitations. You are originally
unlimited and perfect. Later you take on
limitations and become the mind.*

RAMANA MAHARSHI

Much of our daily behavior is conditioned by forces deep below the conscious level of our minds. In Sanskrit these forces are called samskaras, which means a conditioned, automatic way of thinking and responding to the events of life around us. When a samskara is strong, we think of it as a fixed part of the personality. Othello *is* jealous, Hamlet indecisive, Macbeth ambitious; that, we say, is their nature. To many biologists, this is something that is built into our very genes.

I do not agree. The samskaras themselves – jealousy, vacillation, competition – are not permanent mental furniture; they are a process. A samskara is a thought repeated over and over a thousand times, leading to words repeated a thousand times, resulting in action repeated a thousand times. At the beginning it is only a burgeoning habit of thought; you do not necessarily act on it. But once it becomes rigid, a samskara dictates behavior. It is possible, through the practice of meditation and the other disciplines, to go against these conditioned ways of thinking and actually change ourselves from the inside out.

It is the mind that makes one wise
or ignorant, bound or emancipated.

SRI RAMAKRISHNA

Samskaras are like ditches in the mind. They have to be dug laboriously. But they can also be filled in and new channels can be dug. Take resentment for example. It does not burst full-blown into the mind; it grows. At first you simply expect people to behave towards you in a particular way. If they behave in their own way instead, you get surprised, then irritated. The samskara is digging its little channel in consciousness.

In the early stages, this channel may be only an inch or so deep. Thought may flow down it, but it may also flow somewhere else. Also, the walls are still soft and crumbly; they may cave in and fill the channel a little – for example, when someone you dislike says something kind. There is an element of choice. But every time we respond to a situation with resentment, the channel gets a little deeper. Finally there is a huge Grand Canal in the mind. Then anything at all is enough to provoke a conditioned resentful response. Consciousness pours down the sluice of least resistance.

We can dig new samskaras – kind ways of thinking instead of resentful ones, patience instead of anger. Every time you try to return goodwill for ill will, love for hatred, you have dug your new, beneficial samskara a little deeper. Transforming character, conduct, and consciousness is not a moral problem. It's an engineering problem.

*In every veil you see, the Divine Beauty
is concealed, making every heart a slave to
Him. In love to Him the heart finds its life;
in desire for Him, the soul finds its happiness.
The heart which loves a fair one here, though
it knows it not, is really His lover.*

JAMI

It is very difficult for most of us to understand to
what extent our love can be expanded. Everybody has a few people with whom he can be very
chummy, with whom she can be very tender,
but the Lord tells us, "That's not enough. If you
want to become whole and never be separate
again, you should have love and respect for everyone."

Jesus said, "What is the special achievement
in loving those who love you? Even selfish people are prepared to do that. Bless those that curse
you." I can see the twinkle in his eye as the gathering gasps. This is the daring of Jesus. Today we
talk about revolution, but I think there has never
been a greater revolutionary than Jesus the
Christ. He tells us that by loving those who hate
us, we can win our freedom, because we will no
longer be dependent on how others act towards
us. The person who practices this can reach the
summit of human consciousness, for it is only
by loving people who oppose us and learning to
bear with them that we can heal ourselves and
heal them too.

There is no greater glory than love,
nor any greater punishment than jealousy.

LOPE DE VEGA

It is good to admire beauty, but it is neither good nor practical to want to take beauty home, put it on the mantle, and say, "You stay right there." When we see something beautiful, we may begin to want it for ourselves. It may be a dramatic house, it may be a lovely flower, it may be a graceful dancer – we just want it. If this wanting becomes a compulsion, it is likely we will lose what we want so much.

Jealousy comes into a relationship when we try to possess someone for ourselves. It is a very difficult secret to discover: that when we do not want to possess another person selfishly, when we do not make demand after demand, the relationship will grow and last. And it is something we have to learn the hard, hard way. This is the secret of all relationships, not only between husband and wife, boyfriend and girlfriend, but between friend and friend, parents and children. Instead of trying to exact and demand, just give, and give more, and give still more. This is the way to earn love and respect.

*Love feels no burden, thinks nothing of
trouble, attempts what is above its strength.
. . . It is therefore able to undertake all
things, and it completes many things, and
warrants them to take effect, where he who
does not love, would faint and lie down.*

THOMAS A KEMPIS

Without a tank full of gas, no car can drive very far. The mind, too, needs a full tank of vitality to draw on for patience, resilience, and creativity. Filling that tank every morning is one of the most practical purposes of meditation. The test of your meditation is: How long can you go on putting those around you first? In the beginning, you should aim to make it at least to noon acting like the proverbial angel.

Most of us, however, even if we start with a full tank, have little control over the thousand and one little pinpricks that drain vitality as we go along: worry, vacillation, irritation, daydreaming, dwelling on ourselves. By lunchtime the indicator may be hovering around empty.

Then it is that you have to be acutely vigilant. The tank is nearly empty, but by sheer effort and deft defensive driving, using the mantram, you manage to coast through to the end of the day without any serious accidents.

The more effort you make, the more endurance you gain. The next day you may sit down for meditation and find the tank itself a little larger; you start the next day with a greater capacity for love and patience than before.

*We must do our business faithfully,
without trouble or disquiet, recalling
our mind to God mildly, and with
tranquillity, as often as we find it
wandering from Him.*

BROTHER LAWRENCE

It is very important to go through the words of the meditation passage *slowly*. You are trying to put a brake on the restless rush of the mind.

A fast mind is like a race car in the hands of a dubious driver. Fear, resentment, greed, anger, self-will, and jealousy rush through the mind at a hundred miles an hour. At such speeds we cannot turn, stop, or keep from crashing into people. At speeds like this we are not really driving at all. We are hostages, trussed up in the trunk. And who knows who is at the wheel?

The function of meditation is twofold: it slows the mind, and by absorbing the words of an inspirational passage deep into consciousness, it gradually transforms negative emotions into positive states of mind. The slower the thoughts go, the greater the control you have over them, and the more positive they become.

As pure water poured into pure water
Becomes the very same, so does the Self
Of the illumined man or woman verily
Become one with the Godhead.

KATHA UPANISHAD

For some reason, it is very difficult for us to accept our divine nature. This has always puzzled me. We pay money for books about how destructive we are. We stand in line to see movies that emphasize our capacity for making trouble. We go to encounter groups where we agitate each other over our weaknesses. Then, when Jesus comes to tell us that the kingdom of heaven is within us, we say, "There must be some mistake."

It is to convince us that our real Self is always pure and eternal that men and women of God keep arising among us. More than anything, we need to hear their good news that the source of all joy and security is right within. In the Hindu scriptures there is a precise term for our real nature: the Atman. All it means is "the Self" – not the little self, the changing personality with which most of us identify, but the higher Self, our real, changeless personality, which we discover in the depths of meditation.

*Nothing is more beautiful than the love
that has weathered the storms of life. . . .
The love of the young for the young, that is
the beginning of life. But the love of the
old for the old, that is the beginning of
– of things longer.*

JEROME K. JEROME

Every morning, just after you step on the bathroom scale to make sure you haven't put on an
extra ounce when you weren't looking, you can
step on the scale of love and make sure your ego
hasn't put on any weight. The critical measure is
your capacity to be equable and kind in everyday relationships.

We all tend to feel impatient when something
we want is waiting round the corner; and we all
occasionally get angry when that something
slips away. The positive approach is to be aware
enough of this cycle to say sincerely, "Tomorrow I am going to be a little more patient than I
was today. The day after, I am going to be a little
more self-controlled." Working on equability
every day yields results.

Where intimate relationships are concerned,
your love should grow. Don't ever be satisfied
with telling your partner, "I love you every bit as
much as that first time I saw you going up the es-
calator in Macy's!" Love should never be static;
it must never become stagnant. Fifty years after
Macy's you should be able to say, "I love you
fifty times more than I did that first day." That is
true love speaking.

Thoughts of themselves have no substance;
let them arise and pass away unheeded.
Thoughts will not take form of themselves,
unless they are grasped by the attention;
if they are ignored, there will be no
appearing and no disappearing.

ASHVAGHOSHA

Life is a kind of play in which we are called upon to play our part with skill. But in meditation we are sometimes more like the audience, while our thoughts are the actors. Anger is there wearing his long fangs. Fear is rattling his chains. Jealousy is admiring herself in the mirror and smearing on green mascara.

Now, these thought-actors are like actors and actresses everywhere: they thrive on a responsive audience. When Jealousy comes out on stage and we sit forward on our seats, all eyes, she really puts on a show. But on the other hand, what happens if nobody comes to see the performance?

No actor likes to play to an empty house. If they're real professionals, they might give their best for a couple of nights, but after that they're bound to get a little slack. Jealousy doesn't bother with her makeup any more; who's going to admire it? Anger throws away his fangs. Fear puts away his chains. Whom can they impress? Finally, the whole cast gives it up as a bad job and goes out for a midnight cup of chocolate.

In other words, when you can direct attention, your thinking will never be compulsive again.

Existence is a strange bargain.
Life owes us little; we owe it everything.
The only true happiness comes from
squandering ourselves for a purpose.

WILLIAM COWPER

We often think that if we go after what we want, we will probably get it; then we will be happy and secure. The mass media have latched onto this line of thinking and intone it like a litany: grab, grab, grab! Yet sooner or later the whole smorgasbord of things begins to lose its luster. Then the sensitive person asks, "If I go on grabbing and grabbing, at what point do I become secure and feel no more need to grab?" This question can lead to some far-reaching changes in our lives.

Our needs are much too big to be satisfied with things, no matter how many we can manage to acquire. The more we try to get, the more acutely we feel those bigger, undeniable needs. Our deepest need is for the joy that comes with loving and being loved, with knowing we are of genuine use to others. The more we give of ourselves to others, the more the Lord within wants to give us. Every day we empty ourselves by giving all we can in the way of kindness and loving help. Then every morning we will find ourselves full again – of love, of understanding, of forgiveness, of energy.

Love to faults is always blind,
Always is to joy inclined,
Lawless, winged, and unconfined,
And breaks all chains from every mind.

WILLIAM BLAKE

The loathsome mask has fallen,
the man remains
Sceptreless, free, uncircumscribed, but man
Equal, unclassed, tribeless, and nationless,
Exempt from awe, worship, degree, the king
Over himself.

PERCY BYSSHE SHELLEY

None of us wants to be artificial. We all want to be natural and spontaneous, but true spontaneity is not simply doing what we feel like doing and not doing what we don't feel like doing. That is simply reacting as we have been conditioned to react. It is really no more spontaneous than a rubber ball which bounces when we drop it on the sidewalk.

We are being truly spontaneous when we can change the habits of a lifetime. We are being truly spontaneous when we are able to drop our pet project and work for the welfare of those around us without a ripple of protest in the mind. We are being truly spontaneous when we can respond calmly, constructively, and compassionately to a difficult situation. The secret of spontaneity is training. We cannot just decide to be spontaneous overnight; but we can all make these marvelous transformations in our lives if we are prepared to put in the sustained effort they require.

*Love and pity and wish well to every soul in
the world; dwell in love, and then
you dwell in God.*

WILLIAM LAW

Loyalty is the quintessence of love. When two
people tell each other, "As long as you do what I
like, I'll stay with you, but as soon as you start
doing things I don't like, I'm packing my bags"
– that is not love. That's convenience. Loving
somebody means that even when they trouble
you, you don't let yourself be shaken. Even
when they are harsh to you, you don't move
away. Even when they make a mistake that hurts
you, you don't go off and make the same kind of
mistake to hurt them.

All of us are so liable to human error that unless we have some capacity to bear with the errors of others, we will not be able to maintain a
lasting relationship with anybody, which is the
tragic situation that many people find themselves in today. We should never settle for this
unhappy state of affairs. It is possible for each
one of us to change this completely through the
practice of meditation.

Suddenly is the soul oned to God when it is truly peaced in itself: for in Him is found no wrath. And thus I saw when we are all in peace and in love, we find no contrariness, nor no manner of letting through that contrariness which is now in us.

JULIAN OF NORWICH

When we are practicing meditation sincerely, systematically, and with sustained enthusiasm, there will be certain times when the mind becomes concentrated just for a few moments and you feel as if you are getting control over a very powerful car. It is like being on U.S. 101 when there is very little traffic, and you are able to travel fifty-five miles per hour without turning the wheel or touching the brakes. Everything is under control. You go down one lane with no merging traffic, no cars pushing you from behind, and no one in your way.

When you can concentrate on one thought like this, there is no tension because there is no division; there is complete security because there is complete concentration. The Hindu mystics describe this perfect peace as *Purnata*, complete fullness.

God doth not need either man's work or his
own gifts. Who best bear his mild yoke, they
serve him best. His state is kingly: thousands
at his bidding speed, and post o'er land and
ocean without rest; they also serve
who only stand and wait.

JOHN MILTON

I interpret this "standing and waiting" as inexhaustible patience, as bearing with people, particularly in close personal relationships. When everything around us is swirling, when we feel our feet are slipping, we get terrified. We fear that we are going to be swept away, and even with our very good intentions, we are not sure whether unkind words may not come out of our mouth, whether unkind actions may not come from our body.

It is when everything is uncertain like this, when the whirlpool is going round and round, that we must be able to draw upon enormous patience to stay firm and steadfast. Calling on the Lord in our heart by repeating his Name, we find access to our deeper reserves of devotion, firmness, and love.

He that is not prepared to suffer all things,
and to stand to the will of his Beloved, is not
worthy to be called a lover of God. A lover
ought to embrace willingly all that is hard
and distasteful, for the sake of his Beloved;
and not to turn away from him for
any contrary accidents.

THOMAS A KEMPIS

Love is a sacred skill that we must work to maintain. Mystics like Thomas a Kempis tell us that the would-be lover must be a martyr. Put into somewhat less drastic language, learning to bear up under changes in attitude and circumstance with an inner toughness is the best practice for loving. If we do not develop this kind of toughness, our love will not be strong enough to support the weight of close relationships.

One of my quarrels with contemporary civilization is the way it trivializes life. We have very little left that is sacred. In a scientifically advanced era, with the benefit of culture and education, we should grieve to discover that our love barely scratches the surface of life – no wonder, then, that it fails to nourish us. Loving is already something of a lost art.

When we finally realize we are missing out on something sacred, we may no longer know where to turn. Love is so exquisitely elusive. It cannot be bought, cannot be badgered, cannot be hijacked. It is available only in one rare form: as the natural response of a healthy mind and healthy heart.

Be patient. The path of self-discipline that
leads to God-realization is not an easy path:
obstacles and sufferings are on the path;
the latter you must bear, and the former
overcome – all by His help. His help comes
only through concentration. Repetition
of God's name helps concentration.

SWAMI RAMDAS

In difficult situations the mantram offers immediate, effective first aid. When you are getting angry or afraid, or when you feel you have to get your way or you will explode, start repeating the mantram and head for the door. Go for a good, fast walk around the block. Repeat your mantram as if your life depended on it – in some respects it really might.

Walk briskly. There is a close connection between the rhythm of the mantram, the rhythm of your footsteps, the rhythm of your breathing, and the rhythm of your mind. You will find that the furious pace of your thoughts begins to slow down, that your breathing becomes deeper and steadier. By the time you get back, your mind will be clearer. A good deal of your agitation will be gone. That is the power of the mantram. The effect on yourself and on other people has to be seen to be believed.

*Wandering with thee, even hell itself
would be to me a heaven of bliss.*

SITA, TO RAMA (RAMAYANA)

For the long spiritual journey, ongoing support, guidance, and inspiration are necessary for everyone. We all need the support of people who share our aspirations, and to whom we can turn in difficult times. So we should not overlook the importance of spiritual companionship, which is a vital part of the eight-point program.

Meditating regularly with two or three friends gives tremendous support. When husband and wife practice meditation together, they strengthen one another immeasurably. The challenges of the spiritual life become so much easier to bear when we can face them with the support of those we love.

But if we find that we must meditate alone, and if there seems to be no one to share our interest in the spiritual life, the important thing is to be patient – to have faith that we will eventually find the spiritual companions that we need. Until then, we can turn to a few invaluable books in which spiritual aspirants share their experiences. These books can become old friends: the writings of Swami Ramdas, the *Gospel of Sri Ramakrishna*, the works of Saint Teresa of Avila, *Of the Imitation of Christ*, to give a few examples out of a vast storehouse of spiritual wisdom.

When you move amidst the world of sense,
free from attachment and aversion alike,
there comes the peace in which all sorrows
end, and you live in the wisdom of the Self.

SRI KRISHNA (BHAGAVAD GITA)

The grace of God sometimes comes in the form of sorrow. If we are not prepared to realize the unity of life, the Lord in his infinite love will let us suffer until we are forced to change our ways.

Of course, it isn't at all easy to change: often it is quite painful. It's very much like learning to use a stiff arm again. If your arm has been injured, and twisted into a rigid position, even the slightest movement becomes painful. Yet you have to learn to move it in order to regain the use of your arm. There *is* suffering in this, as there often is in any kind of growth.

We should never conclude that our lives are hopeless, that we can never improve, that we are condemned by God or fate or chemistry or conditioning to repeat the same mistakes. We always have a choice. That is the glory of our human nature: not only that we can always choose a better path, but that someday we will. We can never alienate ourselves from our divine Self, and the whole force of evolution is pushing us towards the divine vision, in which we see ourselves as we really are: united with the Lord of Love within our hearts.

*A human being is part of the whole, called
by us "universe," a part limited in time and
space. He experiences himself, his thoughts
and feelings, as something separate from
the rest – a kind of optical delusion of
consciousness. This delusion is a kind of
prison for us, restricting us to our personal
desires and to affection for a few persons
nearest to us. Our task must be to free
ourselves from this prison by widening
our circle of compassion to embrace all
living creatures and the whole
of nature in its beauty.*

ALBERT EINSTEIN

None of us see life as it is, the world as it is. We
all see life as *we* are. We look at others through
our own likes and dislikes, prejudices and pre-
possessions, desires and interests. It is this sepa-
ratist outlook that fragments life for us — man
against woman, community against community, country against country. Yet the great mystics assure us on the strength of their own experience, if only we throw away this fragmenting instrument of observation called the ego, we shall
see all life as an indivisible whole.

*The soul's impurity consists in bad
judgments, and purification consists in
producing in it right judgments, and the
pure soul is one which has right judgments.*

EPICTETUS

*Before man is life and death, good and evil,
that which he shall choose shall be given him.*

ECCLESIASTICUS

The capacity to discriminate between right desires and wrong desires is very precious. Right desires benefit everyone – including ourselves. Wrong desires may be pleasing, but they benefit no one – again, not even ourselves. The criteria are simple to state, but not so simple to apply in everyday life.

The problem that arises is that wrong desires can be very skillful impersonators. They put on a three-piece suit and a false mustache and present themselves suavely as Mr. Right, the benefactor of all; if they happen to be just what we like, that is only happy coincidence. To live wisely, we need to be able to recognize right desires and yield to them, which is a pleasant but rare state of affairs. But much more important, we need to be able to recognize wrong desires and resist them.

This can be very difficult. We have to draw on every militant instinct we have and take on the desire face to face, like a boxer in the ring. And we need not yield. The very attitude of resisting in the face of a wrong desire is the beginning of good health, vitality, and love.

We can only learn to know ourselves and
do what we can – namely, surrender our
will and fulfil God's will in us.

SAINT TERESA OF AVILA

From what I have seen of life, problems are a repertory theater. We may see all sorts of characters, but only a very few problems are playing all the roles. Self-will, of course, is the most versatile of actors. In fact, in a sense, he is the *only* actor. He can play any part, anytime. He throws us off guard by continually changing his costume, so that we think we are dealing with a brand new problem, instead of the famous ham, Mr. Ego. Today he may star as Alf, The Amazing Palate Craving, tomorrow as Why-don't-you-love-me Winifred.

Give us a problem that we recognize – dressed in a particular costume, cast in a particular role, appearing at a particular place and time – and we know how to deal with it. But the moment the same problem appears in a way we do not expect – say, wearing a false moustache and a fez – we go to pieces. The mind looks through its catalog and throws up its hands: "Boss, this isn't supposed to happen! I don't know what to do."

The mystics say that we have to learn to see the underlying problem, self-will, and deal with it, instead of trying to deal with each individual disguise. It is the only efficient way to make real progress in the spiritual life.

You never enjoy the world aright, till the
Sea itself floweth in your veins, till you are
clothed with the heavens, and crowned with
the stars; and perceive yourself to be the sole
heir of the whole world, and more than so,
because men are in it who are every one sole
heirs as well as you. Till you can sing and
rejoice and delight in God, as misers
do in gold, and Kings in sceptres,
you never enjoy the world.

THOMAS TRAHERNE

In our relationship with the environment, the real power does not lie in the hands of technologists or politicians or directors of multinational corporations. Individuals like you and me make the final decisions about what is bought and sold in the stores, how much carbon dioxide is pumped into the atmosphere, and what is dumped into the sea. Each of us can begin to heal the environment right away by changing our daily habits.

And beyond that, there is another area which deserves our immediate attention: the world within. For each of us has an entire world within, an internal environment as real as the one we see around us. This internal environment has a powerful effect on the external environment: the way we think affects the way we treat the earth. When we purify this inner environment, we are not only making ourselves more secure and fulfilled, but we are also making an important contribution to the health of Mother Earth.

Love, all alike, no season knows, nor clime,
Nor hours, days, months, which are
the rags of time.

JOHN DONNE

Loyalty is a precious quality that we have almost lost sight of today. In personal relationships, especially where sex is involved, loyalty is considered old-fashioned, even unrealistic.

Today, instead of loyalty, almost everyone talks about freedom, especially in relationships. The idea is that if two people come together in freedom, each can walk out of the arrangement. This is supposed to be a complete safeguard against unhappiness. But even where both are free to walk out – where there are no obligations, no bonds, not even any ties – they go on doing this over and over and do not acquire the capacity to love. Without loyalty, it simply is not possible to love deeply.

If we cannot cultivate loyalty, we should not say we love; time will prove otherwise. We should simply use the word *like*. The law of liking is: Like me and I will like you; dislike me and I will dislike you. Love is not a business contract or a trade agreement; love is something freely given.

I think the world today is upside-down
and is suffering so much, because there is so
very little love in the homes and in family
life. We have no time for our children,
we have no time for each other;
there is no time to enjoy each other.

MOTHER TERESA OF CALCUTTA

An obsession with hurry has been so worked into our social system that we scarcely notice we do not have time to love. Everywhere the slogan is "Hurry, hurry, hurry." Yet to be aware of the needs of others, to spend time with others, to speak and act with thoughtfulness, patience, and consideration, we must give time – a lot more time than most of us are willing to give at present.

We all need warm, deep, personal relationships to thrive, but modern life seems to place such a small value on them – compared with the high value placed on money and prestige and pleasure. It is so easy to be distracted and to fritter our attention away in countless ways, until we find we have nothing left for family and friends. By simplifying our lives, dropping less important activities, we allow more time for what matters most. But it is also essential to slow down our pace of living, so that we can free ourselves from the grip of time-driven thinking and behavior.

*Oh my sisters! how forgetful of her own
ease, how careless of honors, should she be
whose soul God thus chooses for His special
dwelling place! For if her mind is fixed on
Him, as it ought to be, she must needs forget
herself; all her thoughts are bent on how to
please Him better, and when and how she
may show Him her love. This is the end and
aim of prayer, my daughters; this is the object
of that spiritual marriage whose children
are always good works. Works are the
best proof that the favors which we
receive have come from God. . . .
To give our Lord a perfect hospitality,
Mary and Martha must combine.*

SAINT TERESA OF AVILA

It is a misunderstanding to think that people
who meditate are selfishly seeking their own salvation or illumination. People who meditate in
the morning and evening are not doing so for
selfish ends; what they are seeking is the removal
of their selfishness and separateness. Every person who meditates is doing so for all of us.

In a home where one person is meditating regularly, even if the rest of the family does not see
eye-to-eye with her, they will share in the spiritual bonus, because she is going to be more secure, more selfless, and more able to put the welfare of those around her first. All of us benefit by
living with someone who does not live for herself. By some unwritten law, our hearts and our
respect gradually go out to her.

People see his pleasure-ground;
him no one sees at all.

BRIHADARANYAKA UPANISHAD

When I was a boy in my ancestral home in South India, the children used to play a game called *kooee*. One little boy or girl would run and hide in a room of the labyrinthine building. Then he would call out "kooee," and we would hear "kooee" echoing from all corners. "Kooee" would be coming from upstairs and downstairs; from the ceiling "kooee" would reverberate. We would race through the halls, tear through each room in search of the one who was crying "kooee." Then at last we would catch her, and the game would be over.

This is the game we are all playing. Some people hear the call coming from the bank. They are quite sure that if they make a lot of money, they will find what they are looking for, but they will never find the source of the echo there. Others hear the call from the haunts of pleasure. Many hear it coming loud and clear from status and prestige. Still others, tragically, seek power that calls to them with a loud voice.

The practice of meditation refines our hearing, so that when we hear the elusive call we will say, "Oh, that is Krishna playing on his flute. That is his game." Finally, we learn how to trace the sound to its source, and say, "Caught you at last!"

Loving means to love that which is unlovable,
Or it is no virtue at all.
Forgiving means to pardon the unpardonable,
Faith means believing the unbelievable,
And hoping means to hope when things are
hopeless.

G. K. CHESTERTON

Every one of us can learn to love without qualifications or reservations. Naturally, we start with imperfections: self-will, self-centeredness, demands, and opinions of our own. But there is no need to throw up our hands as so many are doing today and say, "Let us be separate *and* have a relationship. Here are my duties, here are yours. This is the boundary line. If you stay on your side, I'll respect you; but if you cross over, you're an invader." Wherever people go their separate ways like this, there can be no love. It is not possible to have both separateness and intimacy.

Instead, we start where we are – somewhat selfish, somewhat self-willed – but with a deep desire to relate lovingly to each other, to move closer and closer together. Learning to love requires a lot of stamina and many years of hard work, and there will be anguish in it as well as joy. But we don't have to wait until our love is perfect to reap the benefits of it. Even with a little progress, everyone benefits.

It is enough that one surrenders oneself.
Surrender is to give oneself up to the original
cause of one's being. Do not delude yourself
by imagining such a source to be some God
outside you. One's source is within oneself.
Give yourself up to it. That means that you
should seek the source and merge in it.

RAMANA MAHARSHI

Devotion is a wonderful aid to the spiritual life.
Once we have it, instead of clutching at things
outside, we now cling to the Lord inside, who
will abide with us forever. In him we see the
reflection of the wisest, purest core of ourselves,
of which we were unaware when living on the
surface of consciousness.

When in deep meditation the turbulent fac-
tory of the mind closes down for just a few minutes, we find a soothing stillness which heals the
body, mind, intellect, and spirit. In this stillness
we feel the enormous draw of the ocean of pure
love deep within, pulling us into a union that is
complete peace, complete joy, and complete
fulfillment. Then it is we realize that boundless
joy has been right there within us all the time, joy
that cannot be limited by separateness and does
not depend on any circumstances outside, but is
an abiding legacy that never leaves us. This is
what is meant by everlasting life, which we can
find here and now.

*We know only that we are living in these
bodies and have a vague idea, because we
have heard it, and because our faith tells us
so, that we possess souls. As to what good
qualities there may be in our souls, or who
dwells within them, or how precious they
are, those are things which we seldom
consider and so we trouble little about
carefully preserving the soul's beauty.*

SAINT TERESA OF AVILA

In deeper meditation, we make the astonishing
experiential discovery that we are not the body.
This body is like a jacket that we wear. I have a
brown jacket with a Nehru collar, made in India,
which has served me very well. I take good care
of it, and I expect it to last me at least another five
years.

This body of mine is another brown jacket,
made in South India and impeccably tailored to
my requirements by a master tailor, whose label
is right inside. This jacket has to last me much
longer than the other, so I am very careful with
it. I give it the right amounts of nutritious food
and exercise. Just like my Nehru jacket, this
body-jacket will someday become too worn to
serve me well. When death comes I will be able
to set it aside, with no more tears than I would
shed when I give my Nehru jacket to the Salvation Army.

Roll on, thou deep and dark blue ocean, roll!
Ten thousand fleets sweep over thee in vain;
Man marks the earth with ruin, – his control
Stops with the shore.

LORD BYRON

Alas, Lord Byron, no more! Industrial society's reach has extended deep into the sea. Pollution, depletion of the ozone layer, global warming – these man-made threats are changing the ocean.

In the Bhagavad Gita, Sri Krishna says, "Among bodies of water, I am the ocean." He does not say merely, "I made the ocean"; he says, "I am the ocean." To me, this is the basis of all our environmental efforts, and it accords perfectly with what ecologists tell us about the importance of the sea. The sea supports us, balances our climate, provides a home for whales and seals and dolphins. When we look at the sea, we should remember the infinite tenderness and compassion of God. When we pollute the ocean we are ignoring and abusing that compassion in a manner unbefitting human beings.

Beloved, let us love one another:
for love is of God.

I JOHN

Nothing is sweeter than love, nothing more
courageous, nothing higher, nothing wider,
nothing more pleasant, nothing fuller nor
better in heaven and earth; because love is
born of God, and cannot rest but in God,
above all created things.

THOMAS A KEMPIS

The idea of romance held by the modern world seems to be taken from the marketplace. We are told that love should not be freely given, but that it is a commodity that must be bargained over. Some wary couples are even drawing up "contracts" to specify who will do the dishes and who will wash the car. As long as the contract is observed to the letter, peace reigns, but any breach brings serious consequences. We model our personal lives after our business lives. If it works when negotiating a contract with your supplier, why shouldn't it work when negotiating with your domestic partner?

Yet, no one is content with this state of affairs. None of us really wants to strike back at those we love. We do not get satisfaction out of hurting people who have let us down. We have simply fallen into the habit of brooding on wrongs done to us, until we finally explode. Set alongside divine love, this kind of behavior is a pale imitation. Love means that regardless of what someone does to us, we will not strike back in anger.

Death be not proud,
though some have called thee
Mighty and dreadful, for thou art not so,
For, those, whom thou think'st
thou dost overthrow,
Die not, poor death, nor yet
canst thou kill me.

JOHN DONNE

The only religious way to think of death
is as part and parcel of life.

THOMAS MANN

It is awareness of death that gives meaning to life and prompts us to search for what is deathless. Without this awareness, we let life slip by as if it could last forever. In truth, we have not a minute to waste in selfish, separate pursuits. When we take this fact of existence to heart, we know death to be our loyal friend, always prodding us on.

Death is a kind of major surgery that every creature has to undergo. Every time we meditate we are rehearsing for this moment of surgery, learning that we are not the body, mind, and senses but the deathless Self. Without preparation or understanding, the experience of death is like crashing headlong into an immovable wall. To get through this wall, we need the unshakable faith that our deepest Self never dies.

*Undisciplined love dwells in the senses for
it is still entangled with earthly things. . . .
Disciplined love lives in the soul and rises
above the human senses and forbids the body
its own will. It is modest and very still. It
folds its wings and listens to an unspeakable
voice and gazes into incomprehensible light
and seeks eagerly the will of its Lord.*

MECHTHILD OF MAGDEBURG

In the Hindu scriptures, the Sanskrit word
kama means selfish desire – not only for pleasure, but for profit, power, or any other kind of
private gratification. The opposite of kama is
prema: love pure and perfected, a selfless love
that does not ask what it can get but what it can
give. The first leads only to spiritual starvation;
the latter nourishes and heals.

In Hindu mythology, kama is sometimes
personified as the god Kama, who is a little like
the Greek Cupid. Like Cupid, Kama is armed
with a bow, and he has five arrows tipped with
flowers, one for each of the five senses. Prema
might also be said to have five arrows: five things
we need acquire in order to love. The first is
time. Second is a one-pointed mind, which is the
capacity to direct attention as we choose. Third
comes energy, vitality. Fourth, we need discrimination. And fifth, we must have awareness
of the unity of life.

*Goodness is the only investment
which never fails.*

HENRY DAVID THOREAU

Discrimination is the precious capacity to see the difference between what is pleasant for the moment, and what is fulfilling always. Today we are surrounded by a bewildering array of glittering life-styles and models of behavior, most of which deliver just the opposite of what they promise. We need to make wise choices every moment just to keep from being swept away. For a long time, these choices are not easy. Often they go against the grain of our conditioning. It takes real courage and endurance to go on making such choices day in and day out. But once you begin to taste the freedom that making these choices brings, you will find a fierce joy in choosing something of lasting benefit over what you crave right now.

*I was held back by mere trifles, the most
paltry inanities, all my old attachments.
They plucked at my garments of flesh and
whispered: "Are you going to dismiss us?
From this moment we shall never be with
you again, for ever and ever. From this
moment you will never again be allowed
to do this thing, or that, for evermore."*

SAINT AUGUSTINE

Even after we have decided to try meditation, and have been practicing it regularly for some time, it is only natural that some doubts and fears remain.

Sooner or later, most of us encounter the haunting fear that if we turn our senses inwards, which is what diving into the murky water of consciousness means, we may lose everything enjoyable in life. This fear is one of the most formidable obstacles between us and the capacity to dive deeper. But if we persevere, we will see the day when these old attachments will fall away, almost of themselves, and no one will be as surprised as we are.

Gradually, with experience, our faith grows that deep within us the Lord is willing and able to take responsibility for our ultimate welfare. Slowly we can surrender our personal will to his immeasurably more profound purpose. Bit by bit, we can work ourselves loose from the grip of compulsive emotional entanglements in the faith that our capacity to love and be loved will thereby be magnified a millionfold.

*In truth, to attain to interior peace, one must
be willing to pass through the contrary to
peace. Such is the teaching of the Sages.*

SWAMI BRAHMANANDA

To a great extent our modern life is built on instant gratification: we are conditioned to go
after what pleases us *now*, without even ques-
tioning what the long-term results might be.
Spiritual disciplines like meditation are just the
opposite. They are permanently beneficial,
though at the outset they may be rather unpleasant. In fact, for some time they may be downright bitter.

I once asked my grandmother, "Why
shouldn't we go after pleasant things, Granny?
It's only human. And what's wrong with wanting to stay away from unpleasant things?" She
didn't argue with me. She just told me to eat an
amla fruit.

It was easier said than done. The fruit was so
sour that I wanted to spit it out, but she stopped
me. "Don't give up. Keep chewing." Out of love
for her, I did, and the sourness left. The fruit
began to taste sweeter and sweeter. "Granny,
this is delicious," I said.

"But you didn't like it at the outset. You
wanted to spit it out." That is how it is with spiritual disciplines.

*And ye shall seek me, and find me, when
ye shall search for me with all your heart.*

JEREMIAH

*Thus abide constantly with the name of
our Lord Jesus Christ, so that the heart
swallows the Lord and the Lord the
heart, and the two become one.*

SAINT JOHN CHRYSOSTOM

The mantram is most effective when we say it
silently, in the mind, with as much concentration as possible. Saying the mantram aloud a few
times can help you get started, and it is so rhythmical that it can be sung aloud. But we need not
dwell on the tune and rhythm. Anything which
takes attention away from the mantram itself,
such as counting, or worrying about intonation,
or connecting the mantram with physiological
processes, only weakens the mantram's effect.

The mantram is a force, and in order for this
force to work, it must be working from deep inside. At first, we will be repeating the mantram
only at the surface level of the mind. But if we repeat it with regularity and sustained enthusiasm,
it will take root deep in our consciousness, until
it becomes as natural to us as breathing.

Whatever I am offered in devotion
with a pure heart – a leaf, a flower, fruit,
or water – I accept with joy.

SRI KRISHNA (BHAGAVAD GITA)

We can look upon everything we do, no matter how seemingly insignificant, as a gift to the Lord. If we hoe the garden carefully so that our family – or a neighbor's family, or someone in need – can have fresh vegetables for dinner, that is an offering to the Lord. If we work a little more than is expected of us at something that benefits others, that too is an offering to the Lord. Everywhere, in every detail of daily living, it is not a question of quantity or expense that makes our offering acceptable; it is cheerfulness, enthusiasm, and the capacity to forget ourselves in helping others.

You need not aspire for or get any new state.
Get rid of your present thoughts, that is all.
RAMANA MAHARSHI

When meditation deepens, and the thinking process slows down, we will find that we don't have to think all the time. It sounds simple, even scary, but it is a mighty achievement that yields unimaginable peace. Thoughts are no longer compulsive.

Just as we turn the key in the ignition of our car when we want to go somewhere, we should be able to find the ignition switch in our own mind. When we want to think constructively we switch the mind on, and drive all the way to Los Angeles without any detours or breakdowns. Anger is a breakdown. Resentment is a protracted detour that often makes us forget our original travel plan entirely and then leaves us out of gas in the middle of nowhere. But when we know where to find the ignition switch, we can start the mind out in Seattle on Interstate 5 and drive straight through to Los Angeles. We have a wonderful trip, and when we arrive and our project is completed, we switch the mind off and let it rest.

There may be a certain pleasure in letting the mind wander, but for how long? What the mystics ask us is simple: Don't you want to decide your destination? And don't you want to get there with your body still healthy and your mind at peace?

*O Lord, how entirely needful is thy grace for
me, to begin any good work, to go on with it,
and to accomplish it. For without that grace I
can do nothing; but in thee I can do all things
when thy grace doth strengthen me.*

THOMAS A KEMPIS

One way of representing God is with a holy
hammer in his pocket. When he finds we are
being self-willed, when he sees us going after our
own selfish satisfaction, he takes out this holy
hammer and gives us a gentle rap on the knuck-
les. If we are really good students we shall be able
to learn with just this one small rap. There *are* a
few rare creatures who have this capacity to
learn. Most of us, however, would not be able to
change our ways if the only guidance the Lord
gave us was, "Won't you please consider this
very carefully and act upon it if you approve?"
The vast majority of us go on making the same
mistake over and over again. It is only when the
raps become painful that we bother to ask where
they come from and how we can put an end to
them. We have to be shocked into awareness that
we are injuring ourselves and others. Then,
through all the little decisions we make day in
and day out, we have to work to transform our
sorrow-producing habits into acts that lead to
increasing joy.

*At the center of our being is a point of
nothingness which is untouched by sin and
by illusion, a point of pure truth, a point or
spark which belongs entirely to God, which
is never at our disposal, from which God
disposes of our lives, which is inaccessible to
the fantasies of our own mind or the
brutalities of our own will.*

THOMAS MERTON

The impetus to gain mastery over one's mind
and senses does not come from some Olympian
height, or from a distant deity. It doesn't come
from any monastic rule, or even from one's
spiritual teacher. It comes from deep within
yourself. You have had a fleeting glimpse of the
shining presence within, and in its bright re-
membered light, all your flaws and blemishes
are thrown into sharp relief. You can't wait to
start removing them.

To travel deep into consciousness through the
practice of meditation you must have a huge desire. The onset of that desire is a sure mark of divine grace. To be no longer content to pick up
what is floating on the surface of life, and to want
only the pearls at the bottom of the sea, this is
grace, welling up from deep inside.

*If your heart were sincere and upright, every
creature would be unto you a looking-glass
of life and a book of holy doctrine.*

THOMAS A KEMPIS

The pure in spirit, who see God, see him here
and now: in his handiwork, his hidden purpose,
the wry humor of his creation. The Lord has left
us love notes scattered extravagantly across
creation. Hidden in the eye of the tiger, the wet
muzzle of a calf, the delicacy of the violet, and
the perfect curve of the elephant's tusk is a very
personal, priceless message.

Watch the lamb in awkward play, butting
against its mother's side. See the spider putting
the final shimmering touches on an architectural
wonder. And absorb a truth that is wordless.
The grace of a deer, the soaring freedom of a
sparrow hawk in flight, the utter self-possession
of an elephant crashing through the woods – in
every one of these there is something of ourselves. From the great whales to the tiniest of
tree frogs in the Amazon basin, unity embraces
us all. Lose sight of this unity, allow these creatures to be exploited or destroyed, and we are diminished too.

Most people live, whether physically,
intellectually or morally, in a very restricted
circle of their potential being. They make
use of a very small portion of their possible
consciousness, and of their soul's resources in
general, much like a man who, out of his
whole bodily organism, should get
into a habit of using and moving
only his little finger.

WILLIAM JAMES

We think we are very limited creatures, very
small, good for maybe only fifteen minutes
of love or patience before we have to crack. Instead of identifying with our deepest Self, we
are identifying with some biochemical-mental
organism.

But when you meditate, and repeat your
mantram whenever you can, you will see how
far you can stretch your patience and your love.
You will see for yourself how comfortable you
feel with everybody, how secure you feel wherever you go. You will find that you have a quiet
sense of being equal to difficult situations.

These discoveries give a hint of the heights to
which a human being can rise. Once we see this
for ourselves, we will catch the exhilaration of
the mystics when they say that because the Lord
is our real Self, there is no limit to our capacities.

*I believe in person to person. Every person
is Christ for me, and since there is only one
Jesus, that person is the one person in
the world at that moment.*

MOTHER TERESA OF CALCUTTA

Virtually everyone today believes that it is possible to love only two or three people. When
Jesus talks about loving our neighbor as ourselves, or the Compassionate Buddha tells us to
love the whole world as a mother loves her only
child, we believe it is all metaphorical. Mother
Teresa says, No, it is literal. Two or three people
are not enough for our capacity to love. We
should be able to love everyone – not feel a
vague sentiment for a faceless mass, but actually
be in love with every individual.

*Precious gems are profoundly buried in the
earth and can only be extracted at the
expense of great labour.*

ANANDAMAYI MA

A few days ago I was watching a woodpecker, a
creature I hadn't seen since I left India. This one
had a red turban. While I watched, he came and
alighted on a huge tree. He was quite a small
creature, and the trunk of the tree was enormous. I wanted to go up to him and say, "What,
make a hole in that huge trunk with your tiny
beak? Impossible. Preposterous!" But this little
woodpecker was not intimidated by size. He did
not throw up his legs in despair; he just alighted
and went about looking for the right place to
begin operations. It is the same with transforming consciousness; you have to look for the right
spot. In some people it is a particular compulsive
craving; in some it is jealousy; in some, blind
fury. Some may be fortunate enough to have all
three. Each person has to look for that spot
where urgent work is most needed.

O God! make me busy with Thee,
that they may not make me busy with them.

RABIA

Let me continue with the story of the wood-pecker. Once our red-turbaned chap had checked out possible areas for working, he settled down at what looked like a solid, unyielding spot and started pecking away rhythmically. He didn't just give a peck or two and then fly off in search of a worm, not to return for half an hour. He went on pecking systematically, with sustained enthusiasm, until he was done. I was amazed at his dexterity. When he had finished, he left such a large hole that if he had gone on, I have no doubt the entire tree would have fallen.

That is the kind of work required to transform personality. For a long time, all we are doing in meditation is pecking away at what we want to change in ourselves. At best it is tedious; often it is downright painful. The problem is that we identify ourselves with the accumulation of habits and opinions, likes and dislikes, which we have developed over the years. We think this is who we are, and are not prepared to let it die.

And I marvelled to find that at last I loved
you and not some phantom instead of you;
and I did not hesitate to enjoy my God, but
was ravished to you by your beauty. Yet soon
was I torn away from you again by my own
weight, and fell again with torment to lower
things. Still, the memory of you remained
with me and I knew without doubt that it
was you to whom I should cleave; though
I was not yet such as could cleave to you.

SAINT AUGUSTINE

To deepen our love, to unify our desires, the Lord on occasion gives us a fleeting taste of the joy of union. Once we taste this joy, all we want is to be permanently aware of him in everyone, everywhere, every minute. This intense longing is the mark of any genuine spiritual experience.

At the same time we experience the joy of union, we see clearly the great mass of self-will that weighs us down and keeps us from our most cherished goal.

Yet none of us need feel disheartened. Remember how even great mystics like Saint Augustine almost despaired when they saw how powerful was the pull of selfish satisfaction. That is our human conditioning, and it is no reason to give up. All of us can learn to reduce our excess baggage.

*The Name of Jesus is as
ointment poured forth;
It nourishes, and illumines,
and stills the anguish of the soul.*

ANGELUS SILESIUS

*As clouds are blown away by the wind, the
thirst for material pleasures will be driven
away by the utterance of the Lord's name.*

SRI SARADA DEVI

When we are getting angry, or are driven by some craving, the mind is taking off like a sports car that can accelerate from zero to sixty in a matter of seconds. It's gone before we even know what has happened. What the mantram can do, when we use it regularly and become established in it, is exactly what a power brake does: stop the car quickly. In all loving relationships, one of the most vital faculties to cultivate is a power brake.

When the mind is getting agitated, when angry words are rushing to our lips and our blood pressure is going sky-high, that is the time to step on the power brake; you just touch it lightly and the car stops. Try it! You'll be amazed at the mantram's power in such situations.

Love is swift, sincere, pious, joyful,
generous, strong, patient, faithful,
prudent, long-suffering, courageous,
and never seeking her own; for
wheresoever a man seeketh his own,
there he falleth from love.

THOMAS A KEMPIS

Our English word *love* has become almost impossible to use. We say he's "falling in love" as if it were something that could happen every day, like falling into a manhole. Is it so easy to fall in love?

Listen to our popular songs; look at our magazines and newspapers. When they say, "I love you," that's not what I hear; I hear "I love me." If we could listen in on a marriage proposal with the ears of Thomas a Kempis, this is what we would hear. The man gets down on bended knee and says, "Sibyl, dear, I love me; will you marry me?"

There is a little undertone of this in almost all relationships. This is how we have all been conditioned, to put ourselves first at least part of the time. Most relationships begin with some passionate "I love you's" and some undertones of "I love me." But if we want our relationship to blossom, we'll gradually change the focus from *me, me, me* to *you, you, you.* Then our selfish passion is transformed into pure love.

*The only thing necessary for the triumph
of evil is for good men to do nothing.*
ATTRIBUTED TO EDMUND BURKE

Some of our most trying difficulties are caused by plain old inertia. Inertia shows itself in not wanting to move, not wanting to act – in other words, in wanting to be a stone just lying on the road. It is all right for a stone to be inert; that is its role in life. But it is not all right for you and me to just lie down and try to avoid problems, saying, "What does it matter?"

When I hear the phrase "well adjusted," I do not always take it as a favorable comment. Mahatma Gandhi has said that to be well adjusted in a wrong situation is very bad; in a wrong situation we should keep on acting to set it right. When Gandhi, at the peak of his political activity, was asked in a British court what his profession was, he said, "Resister." If he was put in a wrong situation, he just could not keep quiet; he had to resist, nonviolently but very effectively, until the situation was set right.

Everyone sees the Unseen in proportion to
the clarity of his heart, and that depends
upon how much he has polished it.
Whoever has polished it more sees more —
more Unseen forms become manifest to him.

JALALUDDIN RUMI

As your meditation deepens, there will still be
occasions when you get upset, but you will be
able to watch what goes on in the lab of your
mind. It's like getting into a glass-bottomed
boat, where you venture out onto the ocean and
watch all the deep-sea creatures lurking beneath
the surface: resentment sharks, stingrays of
greed, scurrying schools of fear. You slowly gain
a certain amount of detachment from your
mind, by which you can observe what is going
on, collect data, and then set things right.

Some of the chronic problems that millions of
people suffer from today might be solved by
gaining a little detachment from their minds and
emotions, so they can stand back a little when
the mind is agitated and see the ways in which it
makes mountains out of molehills. Many problems simply are not real; they start to seem real
only when we dwell on them. The thorniest
problems to solve are those that are not real; yet
most of us go on giving them our best efforts.

*A good action is never lost; it is a treasure
laid up and guarded for the doer's need.*

CALDERON DE LA BARCA

In Hindu and Buddhist mysticism, this principle is called the law of karma. The word *karma* has been much misunderstood, but its literal meaning is simply action, something done. So instead of using exotic language, we might as well refer to the "law of action," which states that everything we do – even everything we think, since our thoughts condition our behavior – has consequences: not "equal and opposite" as in physics, but equal and alike.

The comparison with physics is deliberate, for this is not a doctrine of any particular religion. It is a law of life, which no one has stated more clearly than Saint Paul: "Whatsoever a man soweth, that shall he also reap." The working of this law, we should bear in mind, is not necessarily negative. If we sow mercy, we shall receive mercy in ample harvest. If we give love we shall receive love, if we are kind and patient to others, others will be kind and patient to us.

Envy and wrath shorten the life.

ECCLESIASTICUS

All of us have a need to forgive, whether in large or small matters. All of us suffer little irritating pinpricks every day. It is not very effective to analyze these small wrongs and then forgive them one by one. Much more effective is not to dwell on them at all. Whenever a stray bit of wrath arises and wants to talk over some incident from the past, don't invite that thought in, don't argue with it; simply repeat the mantram.

When we can withdraw our attention completely from the past, it is not possible to get resentful; it is not possible to be oppressed by mistakes in our past, no matter who made them. All our attention is in the present, which makes every moment fresh, every relationship fresh. Staleness and boredom vanish from our life.

All things by immortal power
Near or far,
Hiddenly
To each other linked are,
That thou canst not stir a flower
Without troubling of a star.

FRANCIS THOMPSON

The science of ecology teaches us that everything in the universe is connected. We cannot separate ourselves from the consequences of even the least of our actions: whatever we do *here* comes back *there*. This is the law of the unity of life. Like gravity or any other law of nature, you cannot break it; you can only break yourself against it.

If you throw a bottle into the air, it will return to earth and shatter. Similarly, if you act in a way that violates the unity of life – polluting the atmosphere, wasting precious resources, ignoring the needs of others – you will find your health, your peace of mind, and your happiness destroyed. We are not separate fragments. Like all the animals and plants, we depend on each other and on the environment.

During the next few decades, I believe, scientists will be instrumental in showing us the connections between our daily lives and the environment, in helping us find noninvasive, nonpolluting alternative energy sources, and in exploring and defending the world's great resources. Today we need good science more than ever. Yet we must exercise extreme vigilance – for though science is a useful servant, it is a terrible master.

He does much who loves God much, and he
does much who does his deed well, and he
does his deed well who does it rather for the
common good than for his own will.

THOMAS A KEMPIS

We needn't rule out the exchange of useful, thoughtful gifts at Christmas, but when we expect something in return, it is not a gift, but a contract. Using this strict definition, we might wonder if all of those packages under the Christmas tree are really gifts.

Rather than giving expensive, perhaps not really useful gifts, there are so many more meaningful things that all of us can give. If you have been a smoker, you can give it up – not as an act of self-denial, but as a loving gift to your family. It will be a most precious, most treasured gift. If you have been drinking heavily, you can give up alcohol as an act of love. It is a gift that will keep on giving. If you have been overeating, you can start eating nutritious food in temperate quantities, and exercising regularly. It's a beautiful gift for everybody in the family. These are real gifts.

Know that when thou learnest to lose thy self
Thou wilt reach the Beloved.
There is no other secret to be revealed,
And more than this is not known to me.

ANSARI

To know completely, the knower has actually to become one with the known. To know you as you really are, I must somehow get out of my own shoes and step into yours. I must get myself out of the way in order to know you as you really are. This is what we catch some glimpse of in totally faithful love, where we forget ourselves completely in the happiness of another. The mystics of all faiths and all ages testify that then we know directly, intuitively what the needs of the other are, and we do our utmost to make sure those needs are fulfilled. It is this direct awareness that we can develop through the sustained and enthusiastic practice of meditation.

Amor saca amor.

SAINT TERESA OF AVILA

The mystics are the world's greatest authorities on love. When Saint Teresa says, "Love begets love," she is giving us the precious secret. One of the most beautiful things about love is that even today it cannot be purchased. It cannot be stolen; it cannot be ransomed; it cannot be cajoled; it cannot be seduced. *Amor saca amor:* only genuine love begets love.

All of us have been conditioned, even though we may not put it in such crass terms, to believe that if you love me six units, I should love you at most six units in return. I can feel secure in loving you six units because you have already committed yourself that far. But if you get annoyed with me and stomp out, slamming the door, I should pull back, at least temporarily, my six units of love. Saint Teresa would say uncompromisingly, "Don't pretend that this is love. It falls more accurately under the heading of commerce."

Everyone can learn to love and urgently needs to learn to love. After all, even if you don't learn Esperanto, your life is not necessarily going to be dull and drab. But if you do not learn how to love, everywhere you go you are going to suffer.

Give all thou canst; high
Heaven rejects the lore
Of nicely-calculated less or more.

WILLIAM WORDSWORTH

This morning, when I was reading an important New York paper, I noticed an article on "the dynamics of gift-giving." This article quoted a distinguished professor of sociology as saying that in every gift there is a reciprocal relationship, even if it is not conscious. In other words, when you are making a gift, you are expecting a gift in return.

Not only that, there are very subtle social gradations: gifts to longtime friends, to recent friends, to acquaintances, to possible benefactors. All these factors come into play when choosing the gift. No wonder shopping for gifts is so terribly time-consuming. No wonder people feel confused and inadequate about "What to give?"

But the spiritual approach is very simple. Whatever you give – it may be a check to a worthy cause, it may be clothes to a person who is cold, it may be food to the hungry, it may be medical help to the sick – do it without thinking of getting anything in return. Do it as a service to God, not reluctantly, but with joy. That is a real gift.

What I needed most was to love and to be
loved. I rushed headlong into love, eager to
be caught. Happily I wrapped those painful
bonds around me; and sure enough,
I would be lashed with the red-hot pokers
of jealousy, by suspicions and fear,
by bursts of anger and quarrels.

SAINT AUGUSTINE

Even in the most intimate of personal relationships, most of us still live inside our own private mental worlds. Our attention is often preoccupied – sometimes more in the past and future than the present – so that we have very little attention to give to those we want to love. Despite our best intentions to draw closer, all kinds of distracting thoughts – likes and dislikes, attachments and aversions, private moods, dreams and desires – come in any time they like, keeping other people at a distance. We yearn for closeness and find, more often, disappointment.

Here Augustine echoes the experiences that almost all of us go through, starting often in our adolescence. The journey into deeper consciousness is one we must take up if ever we are to find the love, the closeness, and the fulfillment we all so earnestly desire.

As human beings, our greatness lies not so much in being able to remake the world – that is the myth of the "atomic age" – as in being able to remake ourselves.

MAHATMA GANDHI

If we have a particular weakness, life has an uncanny way of trying us at just that vulnerable spot. The man who is anger-prone finds himself forced to work with aggravating people. The woman who has never learned to control her taste buds can find no job but one as a pastry cook.

This can seem like sheer perversity on a cosmic scale, until we catch sight of the tremendous opportunity it provides. Between our inner need for growth and our external circumstances, a kind of dovetailing can often be detected. There almost seems to be a master hand behind it all, thrusting us time and time again into the same frustrating situation, until finally we relent: "All right, you win – I'll grow if you insist!" This is all that is really expected of us. Once we have made the firm resolve to get ourselves out of the old trap, we will be amazed how quickly our circumstances begin to change, how quickly new opportunities open up for us.

*Love has no errors, for all errors
are the want of love.*

WILLIAM LAW

Without a sincere effort to get ourselves out of the way, we can't understand the needs of the people closest to us; we simply can't see them clearly. Often, for example, good parents have goals for their children that their children do not share, goals that may not be in anyone's best interests.

The summer I finished high school, living as I did as part of a large clan, I was barraged by opinions – from uncles, aunts, brothers-in-law, everybody – about what I ought to do with the rest of my life. The only person who didn't try to put pressure on me was my grandmother; she kept her counsel to herself.

My grandmother never heard of educational psychology – or, for that matter, of any other kind of psychology. But at the very end of summer vacation as I was taking leave of my family to go off to college, she called me over to her and whispered in my ear, "Follow your own star."

*Knowledge of ourselves teaches us whence
we come, where we are and whither we are
going. We come from God and we are in
exile; and it is because our potency
of affection tends towards God that
we are aware of this state of exile.*

JAN VAN RUYSBROECK

Like the story of the prodigal son in the Bible, in India we tell a simple story of a prince who is kidnapped by robbers when he is very young. He forgets all about the palace, even about his father and mother. He just grows up as a bandit, learning to master the bow and arrow, ambush passers-by, and disappear without getting caught.

Then one day the king's spiritual teacher happens by. Many years have passed; the little child is a grown man, rough and cocksure. But the teacher recognizes him, and with great love embraces him, and calls him "your royal highness." The young man, outraged, pushes him away.

But the teacher's faith is unshaken. He begins to tell the young man stories about his childhood, how life used to be in the palace. Gradually the prince begins to remember. Finally, his memory clears. He draws himself up: "Now I recall," he says slowly, as if awakening from a dream. "I'm not a bandit. I simply forgot who I was." Truly a prince, he goes home to his father and mother.

We are all children of God, but we've forgotten who we are.

Let the wise guard their thoughts, which are difficult to perceive, which are extremely subtle, which wander at will. Thought which is well guarded is the bearer of happiness.

THE BUDDHA

After many years of repetition, the mantram becomes an integral part of consciousness. The person who becomes established in this state carries the Lord with him wherever he goes. Sri Ramakrishna says that such a person is like an office worker who retires on his pension after many years of working with the company: he doesn't have to work any more, but he still receives his check every month in the mail.

After many years of making an effort to repeat the mantram, it becomes as much a part of you as your breathing or the beat of your heart. Then you don't have to work at it; it will go on unceasingly of itself. Then, with no conscious effort on your part, instead of being under constant bombardment by intrusive thoughts – of chocolate sundaes, of how unkind your partner was this morning, of that new sports car, of how you wished you hadn't been so rude to the short-tempered waitress at lunch – your mind will be riveted on the highest ideal you can conceive of.

Ah! would the heart
but be a manger for the birth,
God would become once more
a little child of earth.
Immeasurable is the Highest!
Who but knows it?
And yet a human heart
can perfectly enclose it.

ANGELUS SILESIUS

In one of his inimitable images, Sri Ramakrishna says that a great incarnation is like a mighty ship that takes people across the sea. Jesus the Christ, the Buddha, and Sri Krishna can be compared to the *Queen Elizabeth*, able to cross the sea of life to what the Buddha calls the "other shore," beyond change and death. But little people like you or me can at least serve as catamarans.

Catamaran is a Tamil word that has passed into English: *kattu* means to tie, *mara* means wooden planks. We don't have the spiritual capital to build a big ocean liner, but we can improvise by picking up a few planks, maybe a piece of driftwood or two, and tying it all together well enough to float on the sea. That way we may at least be able to carry across our families and friends. Nobody has an excuse to say he or she lacks the wherewithal to cross the sea of life; we can always go on a catamaran.

*We are celebrating the feast of the Eternal
Birth which God the Father has borne and
never ceases to bear in all Eternity. . . . But if
it takes not place in me, what avails it?
Everything lies in this, that it
should take place in me.*

MEISTER ECKHART

The Lord of Love, immortal and infinite, comes
as a divine incarnation in times of great crisis to
rescue mankind from disaster. Sri Krishna, the
Compassionate Buddha, and Jesus the Christ
are supreme examples. In age after age, whenever violence and hatred threaten the world, the
Lord comes down to inspire and protect those
who turn to him, who live in harmony with the
law of unity. He comes to protect such people
from the heavy odds ranged against them, and to
reestablish peace on earth and goodwill among
all.

Yet there is another level on which this divine
birth can take place. Every one of us has this
choice: Shall I prepare for the divine birth to take
place in my consciousness by abolishing my
own selfishness? It is up to you and me to keep
our doors open, to put up a little sign, "Ready
for receiving an incarnation." But our house
must not be cluttered up. It must be empty of
selfishness and self-will. Only then can the
blessed child be born in our humble hearts.

*Little by little, through patience
and repeated effort, the mind
will become stilled in the Self.*

SRI KRISHNA (BHAGAVAD GITA)

Let me compare meditation to driving, something everyone understands. In meditation, as we go through the words of the passage as slowly as possible, we are steering the mind gradually into the slow, Sunday-driver lanes of traffic. This cannot be done in a single session. Every veteran of rush-hour traffic knows that you can't suddenly cut across a five-lane freeway into the exit lane without courting disaster. You have to signal and then ease over carefully. Even if you start out living in the fast lane, over a period of years you can find yourself cruising comfortably along in the right-hand lane with your thoughts completely under control.

You may ask, "Isn't it better to travel in the fast lane? Won't we reach our destination faster and have more fun, too?" The answer is no, for when our car is speeding out of control, we are more than likely to crash. To crash means to get angry and possessive and jealous and hostile, which we all agree is no fun at all. There *are* rare occasions when it is necessary to put your foot down hard on the accelerator, but when the mind is trained, you can do so without danger.

*Death is like an arrow that is already
in flight, and your life lasts
only until it reaches you.*

GEORG HERMES

*The last enemy that shall be
destroyed is death.*

I CORINTHIANS

Most of us find the death of another person or creature deeply unsettling, yet after a time we manage to submerge our feelings and carry on. For someone deeply sensitive to the transitory nature of life, however, an encounter with death can leave scars that last a lifetime. As a teenager Saint Augustine witnessed the untimely death of a bosom friend, and suddenly a trapdoor opened into deeper awareness. He was devastated. "I thought death suddenly capable of devouring all men, because he had taken this loved one."

The word *anxiety* is a weak term for expressing this continuing uneasiness, this unsettled sense of being out of place and running out of time. Generally we can only ascribe it to external events, if we succeed in linking it to anything at all. But what is actually happening is that a wisp of memory is rising, whispering to us from deep within that nothing external in life is secure, nothing physical ever lasts.

An encounter with death, as in the case of Augustine, can leave us changed for the better. It can prompt us forward on the long search for something secure in life, something death cannot reach.

*Reason is like an officer when the King
appears. The officer then loses his power and
hides himself. Reason is the shadow
cast by God; God is the sun.*

JALALUDDIN RUMI

Thinking, however useful it may be at times, is
not the highest human faculty; it is only a stage
in development. If, for example, in the throes of
evolution we had stopped with instinct, saying,
"This is the highest possible mode of knowing,"
our human future would have been stunted: I
would not be seated here writing these words,
nor would you be reading them.

Like instinct, reason is only a way station.
When friends and I go to Berkeley to see a play,
we sometimes stop halfway along to stretch our
legs. But we don't get so involved in stretching
legs that we forget to go on to the theater.
Thought is a useful but temporary stopping station; it should not be considered a permanent
solution to the problems of living. Just as we
were able to rise above instinct and to develop
reason, the mystics say we must one day pass beyond discursive thinking and enter into a higher
mode of knowing.

The Buddha said that we cannot solve the
problems of the mind with the mind. We cannot
solve our problems by thinking about them, analyzing them, talking about them. In meditation, we often simply leave personal problems
behind – we move out of the neighborhood
where they live.

Out of compassion I destroy the darkness
of their ignorance. From within them I light
the lamp of wisdom and dispel all
darkness from their lives.

SRI KRISHNA (BHAGAVAD GITA)

With infinite tenderness, the Lord lets it dawn on us only gradually that we are not separate, that we belong entirely to him. If this realization were to come overnight, ordinary people like you and me would not be able to withstand it; it would be more than our nervous systems could bear. That is why the Lord is so gentle with us; he spreads the transformation from separateness to unity out over many years so that all these changes in the mind and body can take place gradually. Often we are not even aware they are taking place until we look back and remember how we were some years before.

When we are meditating regularly, we should not ask when illumination will come. We should have a patient impatience to reach the goal. Finally, after many years, no matter what our past has been, we will begin to live in the light that knows no night. The temple may have been dark for a thousand years, the Hindu mystics say, but once the lamp is lit, every corner will be ablaze with light.

*On the one hand I felt the call of God; on
the other, I continued to follow the world.
All the things of God gave me great pleasure,
but I was held captive by those of the world.
I might have been said to be trying to
reconcile these two extremes, to bring
contraries together: the spiritual life on
the one hand and worldly satisfactions,
pleasures, and pastimes on the other.*

SAINT TERESA OF AVILA

Saint Teresa of Avila was a remarkably spiritual woman. Even as a girl she could say passionately, "I want something that will last forever!" Yet this woman who was to become one of the world's greatest mystics went through twenty years of doubt and struggle before becoming established in God. If Teresa took twenty years, can people like you and me think of doing it in less? Her words can inspire all of us, for everyone begins with doubts and conflicts. Little people like us are likely to be haunted by them – and to feel frequently disheartened for a long, long time.

When you have doubts about your capacity for spiritual progress, don't be defeatist. Remember these words of Saint Teresa and keep striving, keep on trying. This is all we are expected to do.

Imagine if all the tumult of the body
were to quiet down, along with all our
busy thoughts. . . . Imagine if all things that
are perishable grew still. . . . And imagine if
that moment were to go on and on, leaving
behind all other sights and sounds but this
one vision which ravishes and absorbs and
fixes the beholder in joy; so that the rest
of eternal life were like that moment of
illumination which leaves us breathless.

SAINT AUGUSTINE

As I reach the spiritual summit, I hardly feel my body. My mind is still; my ego has been set at rest. The peace in my heart matches the peace at the heart of nature. This is my native state, the state to which I have been striving through the long travail of evolution to return. No longer am I a feverish fragment of life; I am indivisible from the Whole.

I live completely in the present, released from the prison of the past with its haunting memories and vain regrets, released from the prison of the future with its tantalizing hopes and tormenting fears. All the enormous capacities formerly trapped in past and future flow to me here and now, concentrated in the hollow of my palm. No longer driven by the desire for personal pleasure or profit, I am free to use all these capacities to alleviate the suffering of those around me. In living for others, I come to life.

« *An Eight-Point Program* »

1. Meditation

The heart of this program is meditation: half an hour every morning, as early as is convenient. Do not increase this period; if you want to meditate more, have half an hour in the evening also, preferably at the very end of the day.

Set aside a room in your home to be used only for meditation and spiritual reading. After a while that room will become associated with meditation in your mind, so that simply entering it will have a calming effect. If you cannot spare a room, have a particular corner. Whichever you choose, keep your meditation place clean, well ventilated, and reasonably austere.

Sit in a straight-backed chair or on the floor and gently close your eyes. If you sit on the floor, you may need to support your back lightly against a wall. You should be comfortable enough to forget your body, but not so comfortable that you become drowsy.

Whatever position you choose, be sure to keep your head, neck, and spinal column erect in a straight line. As concentration deepens, the nervous system relaxes and you may begin to fall asleep. It is important to resist this tendency right from the beginning, by drawing yourself up and away from your back support until the wave of sleep has passed.

Once you have closed your eyes, begin to go *slowly,* in your mind, through a passage from the scriptures or the great mystics which you have memorized for use in meditation, for example the Prayer of Saint Francis of Assisi:

Lord, make me an instrument of thy peace.
Where there is hatred, let me sow love;
Where there is injury, pardon;
Where there is doubt, faith;
Where there is despair, hope;
Where there is darkness, light;
Where there is sadness, joy.

O divine Master, grant
*   that I may not so much seek*
To be consoled as to console,
To be understood as to understand,
To be loved as to love;
For it is in giving that we receive;
It is in pardoning that we are pardoned;
It is in dying [to self] that we are born to
*   eternal life.*

While you are meditating, do not follow any association of ideas or try to think about the passage. If you are giving your attention to each word, the meaning cannot help sinking in. When distractions come, do not resist them, but give more attention to the words of the passage. If your mind strays from the passage entirely, bring it back gently to the beginning and start again.

When you reach the end of the passage, you may use it again as necessary to complete your period of meditation until you have memorized others. It is helpful to have a wide variety of passages for meditation, drawn from the world's major traditions. Each passage should be positive and practical, drawn from a major scripture or from a mystic of the highest stature. For example:

★ the Twenty-third Psalm
★ the Shema
★ the Lord's Prayer
★ the Beatitudes

- ★ Saint Paul's "Epistle on Love"
  (1 Corinthians 13)
- ★ Thomas a Kempis, *Imitation of Christ* III. 5
  ("The Wonderful Effects of Divine Love")
- ★ Chapters 1 and 26 of the Dhammapada of the Buddha
- ★ Selections from the Bhagavad Gita:
  2.54 - 72 ("The Illumined Man")
  9.26 - 34 ("Make It an Offering")
  12.1 - 20 ("The Way of Love")
  18.49 - 73 ("Be Aware of Me Always")
- ★ Ansari of Herat, "Invocations"

Most of these passages, along with many others equally beautiful selected from the world's religions, can be found in *God Makes the Rivers to Flow, Passages for Meditation*, selected by Eknath Easwaran (Nilgiri Press, 1982).

The secret of meditation is simple: we become what we meditate on. When you use the Prayer of Saint Francis every day in meditation, you are driving the words deep into your consciousness. Eventually they become an integral part of your personality, which means they will find constant expression in what you do, what you say, and what you think.

2. Repetition of the Mantram

A mantram, or Holy Name, is a powerful spiritual formula which has the capacity to transform consciousness when it is repeated silently in the mind. There is nothing magical about this. It is simply a matter of practice, as you can verify for yourself.

Every religious tradition has a mantram, often more than one. For Christians, the name of Jesus itself is a powerful mantram. Catholics also use *Hail Mary* or *Ave Maria*. Jews may use *Barukh attah Adonai*, "Blessed art thou, O Lord," or the Hasidic formula *Ribono shel olam*, "Lord of the universe." Muslims repeat the name of Allah or

Allahu akbar, "God is great." Probably the oldest Buddhist mantram is *Om mani padme hum,* referring to the "jewel in the lotus of the heart." In Hinduism, among many choices, the most popular is *Rama, Rama, Rama,* or the longer version:

> *Haré Rama, Haré Rama,*
> *Rama Rama, Haré Haré,*
> *Haré Krishna, Haré Krishna,*
> *Krishna Krishna, Haré Haré.*

Select a mantram that appeals to you deeply. In many traditions it is customary to take the mantram used by your spiritual teacher. Then, once you have chosen, do not change your mantram. Otherwise you will be like a person digging shallow holes in many places; you will never go deep enough to find water.

Repeat your mantram silently whenever you get the chance: while walking, while waiting, while doing mechanical chores like washing dishes, and especially when you are falling asleep. You will find for yourself that this is not mindless repetition. The mantram will help to keep you relaxed and alert during the day, and when you can fall asleep in it, it will go on working for you throughout the night as well.

Whenever you are angry or afraid, nervous or worried or resentful, repeat the mantram until the agitation subsides. The mantram works to steady the mind, and all these emotions are power running against you which the mantram can harness and put to work.

3. Slowing Down

Hurry makes for tension, insecurity, inefficiency, and superficial living. It also makes for illness: among other things, "hurry sickness" is a major component of the type A behavior pattern which research has linked to heart disease. To guard against hurrying through the day, start the day early and simplify your life so that you do not try to fill your time with more than you can do. When you find yourself beginning to speed up, repeat your mantram to help you slow down.

It is important here not to confuse slowness with sloth, which breeds carelessness, procrastination, and general inefficiency. In slowing down we should attend meticulously to details, giving our very best even to the smallest undertaking.

4. One-pointedness

Doing more than one thing at a time divides attention and fragments consciousness. When we read and eat at the same time, for example, part of our mind is on what we are reading and part on what we are eating; we are not getting the most from either activity. Similarly, when talking with someone, give him or her your full attention. These are little things, but all together they help to unify consciousness and deepen concentration.

Everything we do should be worthy of our full attention. When the mind is one-pointed it will be secure, free from tension, and capable of the concentration that is the mark of genius in any field.

5. Training the Senses

In the food we eat, the books and magazines we read, the movies we see, all of us are subject to the conditioning of rigid likes and dislikes. To free ourselves from this conditioning, we need to learn to change our likes and dislikes freely when it is in the best interests of those around us or ourselves. We should choose what we eat by what our body needs, for example, rather than by what the taste buds demand. Similarly, the mind eats too, through the senses. We need to be particularly discriminating in what we read and what we go to see for entertainment, for we become in part what our senses take in.

6. Putting Others First

Dwelling on ourselves builds a wall between ourselves and others. Those who keep thinking about *their* needs, *their* wants, *their* plans, *their* ideas cannot help becoming lonely and insecure. It is important to learn to put other people first — beginning within the circle of your family and friends, where there is already a basis of love on which to build. When two people try to put each other first, they are not only moving closer to each other. They are also removing the barriers of their ego-prison, which deepens their relationships with everyone else as well.

7. Reading in World Mysticism

We are so surrounded today by a low concept of what the human being is that it is important to give ourselves a higher image by devoting half an hour or so each day to reading the scriptures and the writings of the great mystics of all religions. Just before bedtime, after evening meditation, is a particularly good time, because the thoughts you fall asleep in will be with you throughout the night.

There is a helpful distinction between works of inspiration and works of spiritual instruction. Inspiration may be drawn from every tradition or religion. Instructions in meditation and other spiritual disciplines, however, can differ from, and even seem to contradict, each other. For this reason, it is wise to confine instructional reading to the works of one teacher or path. Choose your teacher carefully. A good teacher lives what he or she teaches, and it is the student's responsibility to exercise sound judgment. Then, once you have chosen, give your teacher your full loyalty.

8. Spiritual Association

When we are trying to change our life, we need the support of others with the same goal. If you have friends who are meditating along the lines suggested here, it is a great help to meditate together regularly. Share your times of entertainment too; relaxation is an important part of spiritual living.

This eightfold program, if it is followed sincerely and systematically, begins to transform personality almost immediately, leading to profoundly beneficial changes which spread to those around us.

« Suggested Readings »

Of the mystics from the West quoted in this book, almost all can be found in the Paulist Press "Classics of Western Spirituality" series, now the best source for Christian (and some Jewish and Islamic) mystics otherwise out of print: Jan van Ruysbroeck, Julian of Norwich, Jacob Boehme, and many others, including the anonymous works *Cloud of Unknowing* and *Theologia Germanica*, misleadingly listed in this series under the authorship of Martin Luther. Some, true classics, are available in many other editions as well: Augustine's *Confessions*, Brother Lawrence's *Practice of the Presence of God*, Thomas a Kempis's *Imitation of Christ*, and the works of the great Spanish mystics Teresa of Avila and John of the Cross.

Other classics of Christian mysticism are: *The Way of a Pilgrim*, translated by R.M. French (many editions), *The Story of a Soul: An Autobiography*, by Saint Therese de Lisieux, translated by John Beevers (Doubleday, Image, 1957), and *The Little Flowers of Saint Francis* (Doubleday, Image, 1958).

For the Indian scriptures, we recommend the translations of Eknath Easwaran published by Nilgiri Press (Petaluma, California): *The Bhagavad Gita*, *The Upanishads*, and *The Dhammapada*.

Also highly recommended are two basic books by Eknath Easwaran: *Meditation* and *The Mantram Handbook*.

For further reading about Mahatma Gandhi, we recommend *Gandhi the Man*, by Eknath Easwaran (Nilgiri Press, 1977), and *Gandhi: His Life and Message for the World*, by Louis Fischer (New American Library, Signet, 1954).

As anthologies and background reading, we recommend the following: *The Perennial Philosophy*, by Aldous Huxley (Harper, 1945), *Mysticsim: A Study and an Anthology* by F.C. Happold (Penguin, 1970), *God Makes the Rivers to Flow: Passages for Meditation*, selected by Eknath Easwaran (Nilgiri Press, 1982), and *The Religions of Man*, by Huston Smith (New American Library, Signet, 1958.)